D0573633

The Whitetail Deer Hunter's Almanac

Books Previously Published by John Weiss

1976   ADVANCED BASS FISHING, E.P. Dutton

1977   ADVANCED BASS FISHING, Stoeger Sportsman's Library

1978   HUNTING GEAR YOU CAN MAKE, The Outdoor Life Book Club

1979   THE WHITETAIL DEER HUNTER'S HANDBOOK, Winchester Press

1981   TRAIL COOKING, The Outdoor Life Book Club

1982   TRAIL COOKING, VanNostrand Reinhold

1982   CARE & COOKING OF FISH & GAME, Winchester Press

1983   OUTDOOR COOKERY, The Outdoor Life Book Club

1984   VENISON!, The Outdoor Life Book Club

1985   ADVANCED BASS FISHING, The Outdoor Life Book Club

1987   ADVANCED DEER HUNTING, The Outdoor Life Book Club

1993   THE PANFISHERMAN'S BIBLE, Doubleday

1993   THE ADVANCED DEER HUNTER'S BIBLE, Doubleday

1995   THE OUTDOOR CHEF'S BIBLE, Doubleday

The Whitetail Deer Hunter's Almanac

More Than 800 Tips and Tactics

John Weiss

THE LYONS PRESS

Dedication

For my son, Mike, whom I had the special honor of being with when he took his first deer, at age 12. Now, as a young adult, he's in pursuit of his own professional career with a national company in the outdoor equipment field. It's in a state far from Ohio, but he still comes home to the family farm every fall to pursue whitetails with 'Ol Dad.

Copyright © 2000 by John Weiss

All rights reserved. No part of this book may be reproduced in any manner whatsoever without the express written consent of the publisher, except in the case of brief excerpts in critical reviews and articles. All inquiries should be addressed to: The Lyons Press, 123 West 18 Street, New York, NY 10011

Printed in the United States of America

10 9 8 7 6 5 4 3 2 1

Library of Congress Cataloging-in-Publication Data is available on file.

The Whitetail Deer Hunter's Almanac

TABLE OF CONTENTS

Preface

It was in 1972 that I saw the publication of my first feature magazine article. It was a piece about whitetails, it was bought by *Field & Stream*, and for many weeks after, I found it curious that my favorite hunting hat no longer fit. In the years since, I've been fortunate to see the publication of more than 1,800 additional magazine articles. This is my 15th book on assorted outdoor subjects.

Obviously, since the *Field & Stream* article appeared, I've come to know countless editors in the outdoor publishing world.

This particular aspect of my career has been paradoxical because it was Socrates who long ago observed that one does not accomplish much without having his words and ideas regularly honed by flinty critics, and this is especially true in the world of publishing. In fact, most of the editors I've had the privilege of working with over the years have repeatedly demonstrated their skill with very sharp pencils.

However, in the final analysis, I'll also confess that virtually all of these talented editorial technicians, but especially Jay Cassell, who edited the book you're now holding, have made me look a lot better in print than I am when striking the keyboard of a typewriter or computer.

The point to all of this personal background is to set the stage for this book and make it clear from the outset that one cannot possibly see the publication of hundreds of magazine articles and more than a dozen books without having lived the words he puts down on paper. He must have experienced the topics he writes about and traveled extensively.

And perhaps most important, he must have worked alongside many experts in the tremendously diverse field of deer hunting. To me, this has been more rewarding than actually stringing together an assemblage of words because my travels have taken me in pursuit of whitetails in nearly every state where the species lives. I've also hunted most of the Canadian provinces.

But with the exception of my farm in southern Ohio, I've never hunted alone. I've always been in the company of someone who I've been able to soak up information from like a sponge.

The list of these individuals is lengthy and includes many of the country's foremost deer biologists associated with research institutions, universities, and state and provincial wildlife departments. On the list also are the innovative designers of hunting equipment, including all of the major deer call manufacturers, archery equipment makers, and ballistic technicians and design engineers associated with centerfire rifle and blackpowder arms companies. I've also shared deer camps with all of the owners of major camo clothing manufacturers, most of whom first began working on their revolutionary designs not in some lavishly appointed art studio but at the kitchen tables in their homes, using Magic Markers to experiment with patterns on bedsheets. Then there are the researchers with deer scent and decoy companies, which truly display inventive minds. Finally, and often the most memorable, there are the unvarnished woodsman types, including guides and outfitters, who have a special knack for living in the outdoors; most of them can slip and slide as unobtrusively as a wisp of woodsmoke, don't at all mind bathing out of a bucket for weeks at a time, and often reveal the uncanny ability of knowing where a big buck will show up, and when, before the deer itself even knows.

From my many years of field experience with these unique individuals, and in the chapters you're about to read, I've compiled more than 800 of what I feel are the most important tips and tidbits of advice that a whitetail hunter should—must—know if he's to be consistently successful. No matter where you live, how you like to hunt, or with what specific types of equipment, I'm confident the knowledge and insight of my frequent field companions will be highly beneficial to your own anticipated success.

John Weiss
Chesterhill, Ohio
May 15, 2000

Introduction

I have been hunting whitetails for 36 years. My articles about deer hunting have appeared in *Deer and Deer Hunting, Outdoor Life, Sports Afield, Field & Stream, Petersen's Hunting,* and a host of other magazines. For the past 30 years, I have been hired by many outdoor show promoters to appear as their featured whitetail deer hunting lecturer. My long-time column in *Whitetail Hunting Strategies, The Deer Doctor,* has generated thousands of letters from readers over the years. My book *Whitetail Strategies* is considered "the last word" about common sense deer hunting tactics. In other words, I know quite a bit about white-tailed deer and how to hunt them. The reason I have sung my own accolades above was not to brag about myself, but rather to advise you, the reader, of my expertise in this area. It's because of my extensive knowledge of whitetails that I wanted to write this foreword for John Weiss' newest book, and to acknowledge him as a premier whitetail deer hunter and communicator.

John Weiss is the author of fifteen books, including classics such as *The Deer Hunter's Bible, The Whitetail Hunter's Guide,* and *The Venison Cookbook.* He has written countless deer hunting articles that have appeared in hundreds of magazines. He is a profound outdoor communicator. Still, John is not only a seasoned outdoor writer and hunter; he is a qualified whitetail expert who has a unique understanding of his quarry. Few other experts can bring the type of sharp focus to an article or book that John can. John writes articles and books that readers find interesting and useful; the type of tactics that you can apply on your very next deer hunt—successfully. He shares this vast and extensive knowledge in an easy-to-read and understand manner within the pages of this book. With a down-to-earth approach, John provides readers with practical hunting information that will help every hunter see and take more bucks their next time afield.

John takes his whitetail hunting seriously with gun or bow. He hunts deer with a passion. When he's afield, John knows the importance of being flexible and prepared, and readily takes advantage of every changing situation. He's a deer hunter's deer hunter. John

Weiss is dedicated to sharing his in-depth hunting knowledge and skills with others, in order to help them become more successful deer hunters, too.

As you read this book, you'll soon discover you're going to benefit greatly from John Weiss' expertise and down-to-earth approach about deer hunting. Don't be surprised if this book becomes a very important deer-hunting source in your outdoor library. You'll want to soak in its information over and over again—I did.

—**PETER FIDUCCIA,** *The Deer Doctor*

1

40 Opening-Day Hunting Tips

Sixty percent of the nation's annual deer harvest takes place on the first two days of the season. Are you ready?

On opening day, plan to stay on stand from daylight to dark. This is when the largest number of hunters will be afield, and they'll keep deer circulating all day.

1. If there's one day of the year to be on stand earlier than usual, opening day of the firearms season is it. Try to arrive at your chosen hunting location at least a full hour before daylight, well before other hunters begin stirring in the woods.

2. Try to know in advance where other hunters will be parking their vehicles and entering the woodlands. If you know where other hunters are going to be, you can select a stand location or plan a stillhunting maneuver that may cause them to unwittingly push deer in your direction. I call this the double whammy: Not only may your own scouting for sign and trails pay off, but you'll have drivers working for you as well.

Part of your scouting efforts should be spent learning where other hunters will be parked or camped and their likely direction of travel when they enter the woodlands. This can influence deer movements and where you place stands or stillhunt.

3. When you're hiking to or from a stand in darkness, always use a flashlight. Even though a full moon may provide enough illumination for you to see by, a light identifies you as a hunter. Otherwise, another hunter seeing your shadow slipping through the woods may mistake you for a deer; even the irresponsible hunter who might be tempted to fire a round in your direction knows that deer don't carry flashlights. As long as you don't pan the flashlight's beam through the woodlands, but keep it on the ground, it won't spook deer.

4. Whether you're bowhunting or firearm hunting, get into the habit of packing a lunch and staying on stand nonstop from sunrise to dark, at least for the first two days of the season. Deer will be reacting to the suddenly increased human presence in their habitat by endlessly circling those hunters, which may eventually bring them into your stand area.

5. In regions not subjected to intense hunting pressure, try to scout for sign as close to opening day as possible. If you scout too early, the sign you find may no longer be relevant when the season opens.

6. An excellent opening-day strategy is to perch in a tree stand overlooking a prime feeding area. But beginning on the second day, move your stand back deeper into woodland areas, because deer will no longer be spending time in open fields and crops, except after dark.

On the first morning of the firearms season, hunting a feeding area is likely to pay off. But as the hours and days wear on, move your stand farther into deep cover. Deer will no longer enter open areas until after dark.

Savvy hunters always have several stands in place. They don't decide which one to hunt from until they awaken in the morning and check the wind direction. These successful hunters did just that.

7. A savvy hunter has several stands in place for opening day but doesn't decide which one to occupy until he checks the wind direction before leaving camp in the morning.

8. If you awaken on opening morning to strong wind or hard rain, dress for the weather and go to your stand anyway. Other hunters have waited for this day all year, and even the most unfavorable weather will not keep them out of the woodlands, so deer will remain on the move. It's later in the season, when hunters are tired, that bad weather keeps them home.

9. If you're hunting farmland where deer commonly hear and see tractors, four-wheelers, and pickups, have someone drive you directly to your stand. This activity is less likely to alarm deer in the area than is the sight of a human being hiking down a woods road, crossing an open field, then sneaking through the forest.

10. If you're sitting on stand and another hunter bumbles noisily through your area, don't become discouraged and abandon your stand. He'll undoubtedly keep on moving, and any deer that are around will circle and give him a wide berth, never realizing that another hunter—you—is there, waiting motionless.

11. If you wear fluorescent orange during firearms season, you can become less conspicuous to deer—yet still highly visible to other hunters—by wearing several smaller orange garments. In other words, wear an orange vest and orange hat rather than dressing yourself head to toe in a solid-orange jumpsuit.

12. Whether you're hunting with a bow or firearm, opening day is not the time to take the first legal animal that comes along. There's plenty of time left in the season, so enjoy the hunt, be relatively picky, and take the opportunity to look over several animals. It's during the waning days of the season that most hunters begin lowering their standards.

13. Scrape hunting on opening day of the bowhunting season can be highly productive. This is not the case on opening day of gun season, because most states schedule their firearm seasons to begin after the rut is concluded.

14. Waiting on stand all day can be tiring, so periodically stretch in slow motion and alternate between periods of sitting and standing. Also engage in some "think periods" to help time pass more quickly. For example, you might ponder your upcoming Christmas shopping list, classroom material that needs to be

Don't become discouraged if you hear shots ring out repeatedly in the distance. Have confidence in your stand. Your buck may be about to appear.

prepared, or subjects to be covered in your next business meeting. A tiny notepad and pencil stub can be used to inconspicuously jot down these reminders.

15. Opening day of the firearms season sometimes sounds as if there's a war going on. If you're not seeing deer, don't become discouraged and abandon your stand to go investigate an unfamiliar area where you're hearing lots of shots. Have confidence in the stand location you've selected; a big buck may be about to step into view any minute.

16. Especially when you're in public hunting areas such as national forests, be wary of open fields and meadows at the ends of access trails and logging roads. When you scout such areas before opening day, you may find that they're hotbeds of deer activity, with plenty of rub-lined trails entering the feeding area. But on opening morning, that easily accessible place may suddenly be transformed into a parking lot for other hunters' vehicles.

17. If you don't have the energy to wait in your bow stand overlooking a scrape from sunlight to dark, it's okay to take a midmorning break to eat and catnap. Just make sure you get back to your stand shortly after noon. Recent research has revealed that the peak time for bucks to revisit their scrapes is 2 P.M.

18. Whether you're a bowhunter or a firearm hunter, don't worry if you're unable to do any preseason scouting. There's still one

hot spot you can go to on opening morning: the stand you occupied last year! Succeeding generations of deer commonly use the same trails from one year to the next. And even if you killed a buck over a scrape last year, chances are that another buck has since taken over the area and made a scrape there himself. Hang your stand in the same tree as last year in the predawn darkness, and there's an excellent chance you'll score again.

19. Deer quickly abandon their normal routines on opening day of the firearms season, especially if there's intense hunting pressure. Because of this, you're unlikely to have much success grunting in a buck, using rattling antlers, or hunting open feeding areas. Instead, take a stand on elevated terrain that overlooks a heavy-cover funnel or travel corridor the animals will be using to elude hunters who have infiltrated their domain.

20. If no one in your group is seeing bucks by the second afternoon of the season, they've undoubtedly gone nocturnal. Don't continue to be a diehard stand hunter. Now's the time to shift gears and begin staging cooperative stillhunts through bedding areas, or to gather your partners and stage drives.

21. When opening day of bowhunting season arrives, bucks are likely to be hanging tight with does that are just about to enter estrus. In this type of situation, your chances of calling a buck to your location are between slim and none. Try using a fawn bleater to call in does instead; any bucks tending them will follow.

22. If you scout for a stand location within only one or two days of opening morning, don't unnecessarily prune too many branches on your chosen tree. And don't cut too many shooting lanes. Deer will recognize these overnight changes in their living room and avoid the area.

23. Remain flexible in your hunting style. If you're stillhunting and see other hunters beginning to stage a drive on a far hillside, quickly evaluate your immediate area for a narrow drainage, saddle, or other terrain configuration worth watching for the next half hour. Deer that evade the drivers will use various terrain contours to execute their escape, and you may very shortly have a nice buck dumped right into your lap, courtesy of the other hunters.

24. On opening day of the firearms season, one hot spot where you can depend upon large numbers of other hunters pushing deer

toward you is a public campground bordering a large wooded area. You know where the hunters will predictably enter the woodland. So in predawn darkness, drive around to the opposite side, hike in several hundred yards, and wait until first light. Then quickly pick a place that gives you a commanding view in two or three directions and begin waiting. Before the sun clears the horizon, many deer will have passed your location.

25. In the Deep South, the opening days of the bow and firearm seasons are likely to be extremely hot. The region you're hunting may even be experiencing a drought. When this is the case, a prime location to watch at the crack of dawn is the lushest meadow you can find. Deer commonly satisfy their need for water by spending the entire night in such meadows, licking the dew from the vegetation then leaving for bedding areas before the morning sun clears the horizon.

26. When you're scouting an enormous tract of land for an opening-day stand location, search for whatever is *least* plentiful, because deer will be attracted to it. For example, if thick cover stretches for miles and miles but there are only one or two prime food sources, hang a stand overlooking one of those food sources. Conversely, if you see one acorn-carpeted ridge after another but thick security cover is in scant supply, forget about the food; deer can feed almost anywhere. Instead, place a stand overlooking the cover.

27. If you plan to hunt a farm where hunting pressure is light or nonexistent and you know the locations of several prime food sources such as soybean or cornfields, ask the landowner to tell you his intended harvest dates. You don't want to scout a cornfield a week before opening day, hang a stand, and then return on opening morning to find the corn gone!

28. If you take a bow or rifle shot at a buck on opening day and miss, should you consider your stand ruined and relocate elsewhere? Not necessarily. It all depends upon your previous scouting and determination of how many bucks are in the vicinity. If all indications are that numerous bucks are around, stay put. If you're overlooking a well-used trail, there's a good chance another buck will eventually come by.

29. Prior to opening day, scout areas that are free from intrusion and shooting activity by other hunters. Most hunters don't ven-

Use an aerial photo to find the demilitarized zones—places at least one-quarter mile from the nearest road. Most hunters won't penetrate any farther than this, so the deer won't be subjected to as much hunting pressure.

ture farther than one-quarter mile from the nearest road. Take your topographic map or aerial photo and use a colored pen to shade in all the terrain within 1,500 feet of either side of all county and township roads. Now concentrate your scouting on the interior, unshaded terrain. The deer there won't be subjected to undue hunting pressure on opening day. You'll also see recently arriving bucks that don't normally live there but have been pushed out of the 3,000-foot-wide zones bordering the roads.

30. If there's snow on the ground on opening day, the best time to begin following tracks is early morning. By late afternoon, the deer that made the tracks may be miles away; there won't be enough remaining daylight to catch up to him.

31. In most states, fall turkey seasons coincide with the deer bowhunting opener. When you scout for a stand, keep an eye out for turkeys or sign of their presence. Turkeys and deer both eat many of the same foods, and because turkeys have excellent senses of vision and hearing, deer feel comfortable being around them.

32. Since the opening of most states' firearms season occurs in late fall or early winter, weather conditions can vary from one extreme to another. Make sure you have stands in several dis-

Ignore tracks discovered late in the day. You have little chance of catching up with the animals that left them before darkness sets in.

tinctly different locations so you're prepared for whatever nature throws your way. I like to have one or two stands overlooking prime nice-weather feeding areas, one or two stands overlooking feeding areas that deer prefer during inclement weather, and one or two stormy-weather bedding-area stands.

33. The opening day of bowhunting season is often accompanied by warm, muggy weather and swarms of insects. Be sure to use an insect repellent so you're not continually swatting at mosquitoes, blackflies, or no-see-ums. Equally important, make sure it's a scent-free bug dope so deer don't spook at the odor.

34. Especially in the North, the opening day of the firearms season may see a combination of inclement weather and bitter-cold temperatures. This means that freezing rain, snow, and ice may accumulate on trees, which makes it extremely dangerous to

The longer you can remain afield, the better your chances of scoring. This means your clothing choices are just as important as any other factors.

climb into tree stands. Prepare for this possibility by having one or two ground-level blinds that you can use until warmer weather arrives.

35. The longer you can remain afield on opening day of the firearms season, the better your chances of success. The best advice on this that I've ever heard is: "Dress like you're going to spend the day sitting in a duck blind in December in northern Minnesota."

36. Many states have late-season blackpowder hunts; if you hunt with a muzzleloader, there are two important things to keep in mind about opening day. First, the deer will have already been subjected to several months of bow- and gun-hunting pressure, so mature bucks will have long since gone nocturnal. Concen-

On opening day of a late-season blackpowder hunt, the best strategy is to hunt heavy cover from 1 P.M. to 3 P.M.

trate your hunting efforts in and around the heaviest cover you can find. Second, the circadian rhythm of deer (the hours in which they engage in most of their activities) changes in winter, causing them to be most active from 1 to 3 P.M.

37. If you wake up on opening morning to discover an unexpected blanket of deep snow on the ground, reconsider which stand to hunt from. Sudden snowfall initially makes deer nervous, because their territory has undergone a dramatic change; they usually remain in thick cover for a day or two before acclimating to the change and feeling safe again. Don't follow through

with your original plans to hunt a travel corridor or feeding area; instead, go to your bedding-area stand.

38. Many hunters traditionally gather in roadside diners for breakfast well before first light on opening morning of the bowhunting and firearms seasons. Since the air in such eateries is filled with tobacco smoke and grease, decline an invitation to join your pals, and you may ultimately be the only one in your group to fill your tag that day. Instead, bring a thermos of coffee and a couple of muffins from home and eat in your truck. That way you'll remain relatively scent-free.

39. You won't know exactly what color and pattern of camo to wear on opening day of bowhunting season until it actually arrives. Since changes in the color and density of cover can occur almost overnight, make sure you have several different outfits so you can make a last-minute garment change if necessary.

40. A week before opening day, hang your portable tree stand in your backyard, wash it with an unscented detergent, rinse it with a garden hose, and then allow it to air-dry. This will rid it of any odors that may have accumulated during the offseason while you stored it in your garage or basement. If this isn't convenient, hang the stand in the woods (with a cable lock) and allow rain and fresh breezes to clean the stand of human-related odors.

2

48 Little-Known Facts About Deer

These unusual scientific facts about America's favorite big-game animal not only are intriguing but may help you fill a tag, too.

A fawn's only defense against predators is that it's born completely odorless. The newborn is actually safer when it's periodically left unattended by its mother than when it's in her company.

1. A mature whitetail buck makes an average of 225 antler rubs on saplings every fall.

2. Fawns are born completely odorless, which for the first month of life is their major defense against predation.

3. Deer arc ruminants, possessing four-chambered stomachs. This enables them to feed without much chewing so that they can quickly return to the safety of heavy-cover bedding areas. There, the animals can regurgitate the food for further mastication.

4. Using radio-telemetry equipment, biologists have determined that east of the Mississippi, a whitetail buck's home range is 2½ square miles and oval shaped. West of the Mississippi, in those regions where there are wide expanses of open ground separating the cover configurations, home ranges may be as large as 7 square miles.

5. In a nationwide study of whitetail stomach contents, it was determined that the animals regularly feed upon 614 different varieties of plants.

6. Not only is venison delicious, but nutritionists have found that it's higher in protein and lower in fat and cholesterol than any domestic meats.

Deer are ruminants, with stomachs containing four compartments. They're able to eat quickly and then retreat back into security cover.

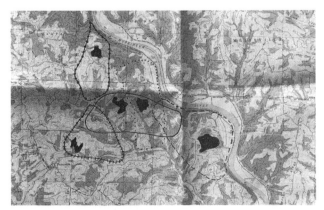

This radio-tracking plat map depicts the home ranges of five different bucks. The blackened areas are their core bedding regions. In the East, most such home ranges are oval shaped and 2½ square miles in size.

In the summer, bucks restrict their activity levels because their rapidly growing, velvet-covered antlers are fragile and tender.

7. The hollow hairs comprising a deer's winter coat are equal in their insulating qualities to the most sophisticated high-tech fibers mankind has ever developed.

8. Bucks restrict their movements in spring and early summer because their rapidly growing antlers are rubbery, tender, and very susceptible to damage.

9. Just because you find occasional piles of deer pellets when you're scouting doesn't mean there are plenty of deer in your area. Scientists tell us that a whitetail defecates an average of 13 times every 24 hours.

10. The "Minnesota Giant" taken by James Rath in 1977 is one of the country's rarest trophy whitetails because it made the Boone & Crockett record book in both the typical and nontypical categories, scoring 199⅝ and 231⅞, respectively.

11. There are more than 30 known subspecies of whitetails in North and Central America, all of which are believed to have evolved from the "type" species. This primary strain is the Virginia whitetail *(Odocoileus virginianus).*

12. No one knows why, but studies have shown that deer respond most frequently to grunt calls and antler rattling when doing so means that they must travel uphill or at least remain on level ground. They seldom respond if it'll require downhill travel.

Unlike humans, deer have a supranuclei ganglion in their brains, allowing them to bed, fall into a restful sleep, then snap to instant alertness in only a third of a second.

13. Ninety percent of all antler rubs are made on aromatic or resinous tree species, such as cedar, pine, spruce, shining sumac, cherry, dogwood, or sassafras. The reason is that the oily cambiums of these species will retain the buck's forehead-gland scent for longer periods of time, even during inclement weather.

14. Research by Georgia deer biologist Larry Marchington has revealed that during a given year, a buck will make from 69 to 538 antler rubs on trees, with a mature buck averaging 300.

15. Deer possess a supranuclei ganglion—also known as an internal sleep clock—in their brains. The mechanism allows them to fall into restful sleep just as humans can. But unlike humans, deer can spring into total alertness in only a third of a second.

16. The size of a scrape is a reliable indicator of the size and age of the buck that created it. Mature bucks paw scrapes that are minimally 18 inches in diameter, and sometimes up to 4 feet.

17. Deer are excellent swimmers and will not hesitate to cross rivers or lakes any more than you'd hesitate to cross a street.

18. The greatest deer-research breakthrough in the past 25 years may be the finding that deer are not limited to black-and-white vision but can see a wide range of colors, including ultraviolet light, which is invisible to humans.

Many believe the biggest deer-research breakthrough of the last two decades is the finding that, in addition to having black-and-white vision, deer can see a wide range of colors.

19. By the conclusion of the rut, an average mature buck will have lost as much as 25 percent of his body weight.

20. Radio-tracking studies have shown that the largest bucks make the largest antler rubs on trees, and they begin engaging in their rubbing behavior a full month before younger bucks do. *Tip:* Find the big, early rubs and you'll have found your trophy.

21. The widest record-book buck rack ever taken is known as "Big Red." Taken in Kentucky in 1982 by Dennis Nolen, the rack scores only 172⅜ but has an incredible 37½-inch outside spread.

22. Hunters who are skeptical about the effectiveness of deer calls should consider that biologists using sophisticated audio recording equipment have identified 15 distinct vocalizations that whitetails make to communicate with each other.

23. For generations, hunters believed cold air temperatures triggered the rut. We now know it's shorter day length and reduced amounts of sunlight entering the eye that cause changes in a deer's endocrine system, spurring the onset of breeding.

24. Many hunters have long wondered why they've never found shed antler velvet in the woodlands. The reason is that bucks eat most of it; what remains on the ground quickly disintegrates. Biologists studying penned deer commonly observe this behavior but have no explanation for it.

25. The largest body weight ever achieved by a whitetail is 511 pounds, by a Minnesota deer taken in 1976. This is followed by deer of 491 pounds and 481 pounds from Wisconsin in 1980.

26. Laboratory studies of deer suggest their sense of smell is at least 10 times more acute than that of a human, and that they are able to separate and analyze seven different odors simultaneously.

27. Can you examine a pile of deer pellets and learn anything from them? Yes! The largest individual pellets are most likely from a buck, because mature bucks are larger in anatomical body size than mature does. Moreover, New Jersey biologist C. J. Winand's research has revealed that a mature buck will leave a pile of 75 pellets or more.

28. When looking at distant objects, the human eye uses binocular vision while the whitetail eye uses wide-angle vision. This is why we are less adept at spotting movement around the periphery of our visual scope than deer are.

The largest deer pellets are left by the largest deer. Each pile that a mature buck drops will number 75 pellets or more.

29. When running, does are far more likely than bucks to "flag" with their tails. This behavior enables the doe's offspring to follow their mothers in dim light or when the mother is fleeing through cover.

30. Eons ago, when North America was largely swampy, deer walked flat-footed with five toes. As the habitat dried, the deer evolved. One toe disappeared entirely, two toes migrated to the rear and became dew claws, and the remaining two toes hardened and became pointed into hooves.

31. When making rubs, mature bucks deposit priming pheromones from their forehead glands. These pheromones induce late-estrus does into coming into heat and also chemically intimidate younger bucks into submission so they are less inclined to attempt to breed.

32. In bitter-cold weather, deer feed heavily upon staghorn sumac. They instinctively know that this plant is higher in fat than any other native food and thus helps generate body heat.

33. Deer have a so-called odor comfort zone of 300 yards. Beyond this distance, foreign odors are not likely to alert or alarm them, because the scent molecules comprising that odor have become diluted and are no longer capable of triggering the chemoreceptors of the animals' olfactory system.

The bucks in this bachelor group are on full alert, having detected a foreign odor within 300 yards.

34. A whitetail's tarsal glands carry its unique "signature," just as fingerprints do among humans. A doe released into a pen with 50 fawns can thus instantly find the one that's hers.

35. Vermont biologist Wayne LaRoche's research has revealed that the width of a deer track—not its length—is the most reliable indicator of the animal's age. The reason is that because a deer's body weight steadily increases with age, the animal requires a progressively wider base platform to support that weight.

36. A doe is able to sniff a scrape, chemically analyze the tarsal scent left there by the buck that made it, and then evaluate the health and virility of the animal to determine if he would be a worthy sire.

37. A lone bed measuring 45 to 50 inches in length is most likely that of a big buck. If the bed you find barely reaches 45 inches and is accompanied by one or two smaller ones, it's undoubtedly that of a doe with offspring.

38. Studies of penned deer have shown that they have an attention span of about three minutes, after which they forget whatever alerted them. Consequently, if you snap a twig while stillhunting, stop and remain motionless for at least three minutes before you take another step.

39. Immature bucks commonly check their scrapes by walking right up to them. Mature bucks normally scent-check their scrapes from 30 to 50 yards downwind while remaining in thick cover.

40. Although a whitetail's home range may span several square miles or more, radio-tracking studies indicate that mature bucks have a core area of approximately 40 acres where they spend up to 90 percent of their time.

41. A scrape is always found near a low, overhanging tree branch that has been chewed and broken by the buck that made the scrape. The buck deposits saliva and forehead-gland scent on the branch to pass along olfactory information telling other deer that this is his breeding area.

42. The reason hunters commonly find pairs of shed antlers near each other is not because they naturally dropped at the same time. Rather, when one antler falls, the imbalance created by the remaining antler annoys the deer so much that he kicks at it with a hind foot, or knocks it against tree trunks, to dislodge it.

Jackie Bushman, founder of Buckmasters, took this buck in the middle of a core area.

43. Whitetails are relatively immune to bitter-cold weather. The species lives as far north as the 59th parallel (which cuts across northern Manitoba and Saskatchewan), where the winter temperatures commonly plummet to −60°F.

44. Unknowledgeable hunters often mistakenly refer to deer antlers as "horns." Horns remain with an animal for its entire life, as in the case of pronghorn antelope. Antlers are shed every year.

45. Whitetails have a vomeronasal organ in the roof of the mouth, which allows them to "taste" odors detected by the nose. After this chemical analysis is performed, the information is then transmitted to the brain for deciphering.

46. The smallest whitetail inhabiting North America is the Key deer *(O.v. clavium)*, a protected species that lives in southernmost

Florida. A mature adult stands only 22 inches tall and weighs 45 to 65 pounds, about half the size of a Labrador retriever.

47. Radio-telemetry research has revealed that, in a whitetail buck's home range, he will lay down his scrapes in a star configuration, with one scrape line having a north–south axis that intersects with a second scrape line having an east–west axis.

48. When a doe enters estrus just prior to breeding, she chases away her buck and doe yearling fawns. After breeding, any doe fawns are permitted to rejoin her, but the young buck is now on his own, searching for his own home range elsewhere. This is nature's way of preventing inbreeding among family members the following fall.

3

47 Time-Tested Stillhunting Tips

How you walk the stalk through deer cover determines how many animals you'll see. These important tips can help.

When you're stillhunting, stop often to just sit and watch. You'll see far more than if you're continuously on the move.

1. Prior to sending his braves out on a deer hunt, Ottawa Chieftain Pontiac admonished them to "walk a little, watch a lot." That advice is almost 200 years old but it's still relevant to today's stillhunting success.

2. It's not necessary to always stillhunt with the wind directly in your face. It can also be quartering toward you from the left or right. Just don't allow your scent to be carried directly ahead of your intended line of travel.

3. Contrary to common belief, midday is not the best time to still-hunt. Most deer are bedded then, and unapproachable. If you stillhunt early and late in the day, when deer are on their feet and moving around, you'll see more animals.

4. When you're following tracks in snow or mud, don't assume that dew-claw imprints automatically mean the animal is a buck. Both males and females have dew claws. These claws show up in tracks whenever an animal's body weight causes it to sink into the soft ground.

5. Light fog, drizzle, or gentle snowfall seems to pacify deer. At such times, they're more likely to feed in open places and for longer periods. The moist ground cover also allows for silent footing on your part.

6. When you're looking into the distance, don't initially pinpoint your attention on a specific place. Instead, slowly scan your vi-

Midday is not the best time to still-hunt, because deer are usually bedded and fully alert to everything going on around them.

sion from right to left and back again, hoping the motion detectors in your eyes will pick up any movement. If they do pick up something, narrow your focus to determine what it is that drew your attention.

7. Always try to stay in shadows and edge cover. Avoid open, brightly illuminated places.

8. A sudden, heavy snowfall will so change deer habitat that it puts them down, causing poor stillhunting. With an entire new world of visual stimuli to adapt to, whitetails commonly remain bedded for two or three days before resuming normal activities.

9. When you plan movements in advance, consider the ground cover ahead. Try to choose a route that takes you silently over wet leaves, pine needles, moss, green vegetation, or slab rocks.

When you're searching visually for deer in the distance, don't pinpoint your focus at first. Instead, slowly scan from left to right and allow the motion detectors in your eyes to pick up any movement that may be occurring.

    Avoid terrain that features crunchy gravel, dry weeds, dry leaves, or brittle branches on the ground.

10. With each step forward, don't put your heel down first. Instead, put down the more sensitive toe region of your boot to feel for unstable ground cover. If you detect a possible "crunch" element, lift your foot back up and reposition it. Once the ground feels stable, *then* transfer your weight to that leading foot; begin bringing up the trailing foot in the same manner.

The Whitetail Deer Hunter's Almanac

11. Be alert to the movements of any other hunters you periodically see in the distance. If you know the probable direction they came from and the direction they're probably heading, you can alter your own stillhunting direction in hopes of seeing deer those hunters are pushing out ahead of them.

12. Soft fabrics such as wool or fleece are far better stillhunting garments than noisy, hard fabrics such as canvas, denim, or nylon.

13. When you're alternately advancing forward and scanning distant cover, keep in mind that you need to travel as little as only a few feet to entirely change your visual perspective and perhaps spot a deer that you couldn't see just moments earlier.

14. When you're following tracks, don't stillhunt directly on top of them. Take a route parallel to the tracks, 30 to 40 yards to one side or the other. Deer commonly monitor their backtrails, and if you're not immediately on the trail there's less likelihood that you'll be detected.

Don't stillhunt directly on top of tracks. Stay off to one side, and keep peering into the distance in an attempt to spot the animal up ahead.

15. Don't spend too much time looking at the tracks, because they only tell you where a deer *was*. Instead, spend most of your time peering off into the distance, in the direction the tracks are leading, in hopes of spotting the animal that made them.

16. If you spot a buck in the distance but he's out of range, don't try to sneak up behind him; there's a good chance he'll detect your movement. If the terrain and cover allow for it, try to make a wide arc to get ahead of the animal. Then wait, motionless, as he closes the distance to you.

17. When you're stillhunting in steep terrain, stay below the crests of ridges to avoid silhouetting yourself against the bright skyline and thereby making your movements conspicuous.

18. If you seem to be seeing large numbers of pellet piles in the region you're stillhunting, don't automatically think that plenty of deer are around. Scientists tell us each whitetail defecates an average of 13 times every 24 hours. Annual harvest figures from your division of wildlife are a more accurate means of assessing the deer population in a given county.

19. If there's a light skiff of snow on the ground, any tracks you discover in midafternoon probably aren't worth following. The

Fresh tracks discovered at dawn are worth following; the deer may be just up ahead. If you discover weathered tracks in midafternoon, though, the animal is most likely far away.

In heavy cover, a set of pruning shears allows a stillhunter to quietly snip away briers and brambles that otherwise will noisily grate against his clothing.

deer that made them likely traveled this way early in the morning and now may be miles away. If you discover tracks at dawn, however, the animal that made them may be just ahead.

20. A set of pruning shears on a lanyard around your neck facilitates silent movement through briers, thorn-riddled cover, vines, and brittle twigs and branch tips. Instead of letting these grab and noisily grate against your clothing, silently snip them one at a time so you can advance another step.

21. Just because a deer looks in your direction doesn't mean that he's actually seen you. Remain motionless and there's a good chance he'll think nothing is amiss and return to whatever he was doing.

22. If you must cross noisy terrain such as a dry-gravel streambed and the weather allows for it, take off your boots and walk the short distance in your stocking feet.

23. If the cover at eye level is thick and impenetrable, don't be too proud to kneel or crawl. At ground level, branches and other brush are usually thinner due to less sunlight exposure, allowing you to see much farther.

24. If a deer sees, hears, or smells you and snorts and runs off, it probably won't travel far. Unlike elk and mule deer, spooked whitetails don't run for miles. Sit down and wait for 15 to 30

Deer have short attention spans, so if you make a sound and a deer looks in your direction, freeze! He may not see you, and in several minutes he'll probably return to feeding.

If you bump a deer, it probably won't travel far. Wait at least 15 minutes, then make a slow arc in hopes of spotting the animal again farther ahead.

minutes. Then begin slowly making a wide arc to the right or left in hopes of intercepting the animal several hundred yards ahead.

25. Keep in mind that once jumped, deer tend to remain in the same type of cover and at the same elevation. If you bump a deer in cedars, it will usually remain in cedars rather than bolt for hardwoods. If you start a deer on a steep sidehill, it will probably remain on that contour level rather than traveling straight up or downhill. This may allow you to second-guess where the animal is up ahead, and let you figure out your approach.

26. When a stillhunt is the order of the day, leave your wristwatch at home. If you become oblivious to the passage of time, your mind won't be distracted by the approach of dinnertime. This will help you to mentally slow down and hunt more effectively.

27. If the weather allows for it, the best footwear for stillhunting is a comfortable pair of sneakers. The worst (noisiest) footwear is thick leather boots with deep lug soles; the exception is when steep or slippery terrain requires solid footing. A good compromise is calf-length, lace-up rubber boots with a shallow, modest tread.

28. When you're stillhunting at a snail's pace, you can't use your regular walking stride or you'll fall off balance. Each step forward should be no longer than your boot length.

29. If it's too windy (more than 15 miles an hour), deer cannot use their senses well and remain bedded. Yet if there's no wind and it's dead quiet, it's nearly impossible for a moving hunter to go undetected. The best conditions see a moderate breeze of 4 to 8 miles an hour. Deer will be active then, and your movements will be covered by nature's sounds.

30. Whenever the wind allows for it, hunt with the sun at your back. This will let you see through dense cover up ahead. And if a deer looks back in your direction, it will have difficulty seeing you because it will be looking directly into the bright light.

31. When it's dead calm—no wind—and you're stillhunting in hill country, you absolutely must be on high ground before 10 A.M. Otherwise, rising thermals will carry your scent upslope to deer on the hillsides and ridges.

32. If there's a moderate breeze, don't worry about thermals. Wind cancels out thermals. Now's the time to work the wind itself.

33. When you're stillhunting during the firearms season, always wear fluorescent orange for safety. But check your state's hunting laws to see if camo-orange is permitted. Camo-orange is readily visible to other hunters, yet its integrated pattern of dark streaks and splotches will help break up your human outline to make you less visible to deer.

34. Anytime you begin to think that your stillhunting pace is slow enough, remember this: It has been estimated that for every buck a hunter sees, at least four other bucks see him first and manage to slip away without the hunter ever knowing of their presence.

35. Whitetails are gregarious creatures that like to keep company with others of their kind. If you spot a buck and are planning how to get close enough for a shot, first visually pick apart the cover for the presence of other deer in the area. You don't want to focus exclusively upon the buck and have another, unseen deer blow the whistle on you.

36. When you see a buck just dawdling around as he goes about his usual business, don't be in too much of a hurry to get into position for a shot. By rushing things, you're prone to making careless mistakes, such as alerting the buck to your presence.

When an unalarmed buck is slowly working in your direction, don't be too anxious to shoot. If the wind is in your favor, he should eventually offer a perfect, close-in shot.

Take your time. Expert stillhunters sometimes work their bucks for an hour or more to get close and set up for the perfect shot.

37. If you know the locations of thickets and other cover where deer commonly feed or bed, and you want to stillhunt them, always try to approach from higher ground. When you can look down and through the cover from an elevated vantage point, you'll see far more animals than you would if you approached on the same elevation.

38. You're firearm stillhunting and spot a buck standing broadside 100 yards away. Do you slowly raise your firearm and take an offhand shot, or do you attempt to move 5 yards to your right where you can take a steady rest against a tree trunk? Take the offhand shot! If you try to move, the deer is likely to see or hear you. A 100-yard shot isn't difficult if you've practiced.

39. Cooperative stillhunts, with two partners spaced 200 yards apart and working parallel to each other, sound like fun but seldom result in success. You focus too much of your attention on keeping track of each other's location and direction of travel. If you hunt alone, on the other hand, you can concentrate on your own slow movements. Also, if the wind, the cover, or the terrain changes, you can make a snap decision to alter your direction of travel without having to consult with a partner.

40. Train yourself not to expect to see "whole" deer. In predominantly vertical cover such as dense woods, you'll most likely spot first the horizontal lines of a deer's back and belly. Or you may detect the unusual curvature of the rump, neck, or antlers. Or the white throat patch or dark eye . . . shapes and colors that are seldom duplicated by terrain or vegetation and allow you to slowly piece together the entire deer.

41. A longtime uncontested axiom is that the most successful stillhunters rely heavily upon binoculars to spot their deer, and not just at long ranges. In close, tight quarters, too, binoculars allow you to peer deeply into the cover and detect deer body parts that might otherwise escape the naked eye.

42. Don't feel that stillhunting means always having to be on your feet, slowly covering ground. If you come upon a good vantage point overlooking a feeding area, brush-choked ravine, bottleneck, cluster of scrapes, or trail crossing, sit down and quietly watch the area for a half hour or more before moving on.

43. Become attuned to the alarm sounds of other critters in white-tail habitat. The raucous flush of turkeys, the barking of squirrels, the scolding of jays and crows, or the thunder of ruffed grouse taking off can all tell you plenty. If these occurrences happen close to you, it's a clear signal you're moving too fast and making too much of a commotion. But if these sounds occur more than 100 yards away, the critters may be responding to a deer that has suddenly come on the scene.

44. When you stage a bowhunting stillhunt, use a backpack-type arrow quiver rather than a bow-mounted quiver. This will make the bow lighter to carry. Its narrower profile will also make it easier for you to slip quietly through thick cover.

45. If you're using some type of cover scent, such as fox urine, on your boot pads, heed this advice: When you stop after every

This bowhunter got his buck while stillhunting near a watercourse.

few steps to view the terrain ahead of you, don't resume your forward advance until you've spent an equal amount of time studying the terrain *behind* you. When deer cross a scent trail, they may follow it out of curiosity to find out what's going on in their immediate area.

46. Biologists say deer are on their feet and most active when the barometric pressure is between 29.80 and 30.29, the wind is from the south or southwest, there's a relative humidity of less than 60 percent, and there's a new moon. You can expect better success stillhunting under these conditions than any others.

47. Researchers have determined that deer seek water at three specific times each day: 7 A.M., 11 A.M., and 6 P.M. These are not arbitrary times but are directly tied to their body metabolisms and cud-chewing periods. If there are water sources in the area you're stillhunting, check them out at the above times, especially during a drought.

CHAPTER 4

48 Trophy Hunting Tips

*Big bucks are unlike other deer. To get one, you'll
need some of these special tricks.*

When you're scouting, carefully study pellet piles. If they number 75 or more and measure 1 to 1¾ inches in length, chances are they were left by a mature buck.

1. Biologists tell us that each time a mature whitetail buck defecates, he leaves a pile of droppings numbering 75 or more, with the individual pellets measuring 1 to 1¾ inches in length. Keep this in mind when you're scouting, because pellet size can help you differentiate between young bucks and potential trophies.

2. A deer track's length has little relevance to the age or sex of the animal that left it. Some deer have long toes (which is what hooves are), and some have short ones. But the width of the track does tell you plenty, because trophy bucks 3½ or more years old have a wide foot base to support their heavier body frames.

3. During the rut, hunt food sources if you're looking for trophy bucks. Mature bucks don't feed much during the breeding season, but since prime foods attract does, that's where the bucks will be.

4. There are more than 30 whitetail subspecies indigenous to North America, each living in a different locale and having slightly different body features that best enable it to adapt to its own climate and terrain. The largest bucks are of the northern woodland subspecies *(Odocoileus virginianus bore-*

During the rut, bucks don't feed much but does continue to congregate at food sources. So find the does—that's where the bucks will be.

alis). They live from Maine to Minnesota and south to the Mason Dixon line. These are the bucks that monopolize the record books.

5. In the early 1980s, the University of Georgia's deer-research facility conducted a series of radio-telemetry studies of hundreds of mature whitetail bucks. The studies revealed that mature bucks create anywhere from 69 to 538 rubs per year, with the average being 300 per buck. Also, trophy bucks were found to consistently rub larger-diameter trees than younger deer.

Biologists have determined that mature bucks make an average of 300 rubs per year. If you've found only a few, you haven't scouted your hunting area enough.

6. Hunt the early-season rubs! To demonstrate their dominance, trophy bucks begin creating antler rubs a full month before immature bucks do. These signposts provide bucks sharing the same range with both visual and olfactory information about the trophy's social ranking.

7. Trophy bucks make an average of 35 scrapes per year. They're nearly always made on level ground, not steep terrain. And they're always located beneath an overhanging tree branch that the buck chews, breaks with his antlers, and marks with forehead-gland scent.

8. If you want to have your trophy mounted, be careful not to damage the neck cape as you field-dress the animal. Also, leave plenty of skin (the entire front shoulder area) for the taxidermist to work with. Although thoroughly salting the cape and head will sufficiently preserve it, it's much better to put it into a plastic bag and then freeze it.

9. When you're following tracks in snow or mud, the presence of dew claw imprints doesn't automatically mean the animal that left the tracks is a trophy buck; bucks and does alike have dew claws. You'll have to check other track features as well, such as the width of the tracks and their direction of travel. Does tend to meander, while bucks walk in a purposeful straight line.

10. Scientists researching the scrape-behavior patterns of mature bucks tell us that the time of day when they most often revisit their scrapes is 2 P.M. Moreover, since it's full daylight then, most bucks don't directly approach their scrapes, preferring instead to scent-check them from 30 to 50 yards downwind while remaining hidden in thick cover.

11. A lone bed is generally that of a buck, but not always. A doe without offspring may also bed alone. To determine the gender of its owner, measure a bed carefully. A mature buck's bed will measure 50 to 56 inches in length; a mature doe's measures 42 to 48 inches.

12. Mapping studies of whitetail travel patterns have revealed that mature bucks living east of the Mississippi have a home range of approximately 2½ square miles. Within this home range, a mature buck will have a core area that averages 40 acres in size. He'll spend up to 90 percent of his time there because of the security that this terrain affords.

13. A mature, virile buck will attempt to impregnate as many does as he can find during the rut. This leaves him worn and gaunt, often resulting in a 30 percent loss of body weight. After the last of the does in a given region has been serviced, a trophy buck

After two weeks of nonstop breeding, mature bucks go into a postrut recuperative phase in which they remain bedded for days on end. Now and for the time being, the best way to fill a tag is to stage drives.

will commonly remain in his bed for a full three days without moving, drinking, or feeding.

14. You've collected a trophy rack and want to transport it home without damage. Especially if you're traveling by air, protect your rack by folding 4- by 8-inch pieces of thick cardboard over the tip of each antler tine. Securely wrap each with duct tape, then give the skull plate the cardboard-and-duct-tape treatment, too. Next, place the rack in a heavy-duty cardboard box and pack it with crumpled newspaper. Finally, wrap the exterior seams of the box with more duct tape and label it with your name and address.

15. If you plan to hire a guide or outfitter to bowhunt trophy white-tails, make sure he's an accomplished bowhunter himself. Many guides are exclusively riflemen, and they aren't familiar with the unique needs and stand setups that archers require.

16. There's a three-week period in the fall when deer love to gorge upon acorns. Stomach-analysis studies by wildlife labs have shown their all-time favorite is the acorn of the swamp chestnut oak, which is a subspecies of white oak.

17. Unlike curious young bucks, which commonly respond to antler rattling and grunt calls by rushing blindly to the scene,

During the three-week mast drop, trophy deer gorge almost exclusively upon acorns to build up their body fat in preparation for the rut. Of the preferred white oak species, their favorite is the swamp chestnut oak, which are the largest acorns shown here.

wise old bucks usually sneak in slowly from downwind. Then they'll simply stand in heavy cover for long periods of time to size up the situation from a safe distance. After rattling or calling, set your equipment down and remain motionless, peering deeply into the thickest nearby cover until you spot your trophy.

18. Radio-tracking studies have shown that mature breeding bucks lay down their scrape lines in a star configuration with a north–south axis intersected by an east–west axis. If you mark all the scrapes you find on an aerial photo or topographic map, you may be able to discern one of these scrape designs. Where the two lines intersect is the hottest location to take that particular buck. It's believed bucks do this so that, no matter what the wind direction, they can scent-check their scrapes from downwind without exposing themselves in the open.

19. Despite their muscular builds and the speedy escapes they commonly effect, mature bucks are lazy creatures. When not alarmed and fleeing from perceived danger, they prefer to walk across level terrain. Very rarely do their normal movements take them straight uphill or downhill. Keep this in mind when you're scouting for deer trails.

20. Monster bucks beyond five or six years of age rarely fight with other males, and their much lower testosterone levels greatly reduce their desire to breed; that's the province of energetic three- and four-year-olds. Once a buck has aged considerably and attained the largest antlers he's likely to ever have, he becomes reclusive. About your only chance of taking one of these monarchs is by hunting the thickest and most impenetrable cover you can find, so long as it's within close proximity of a prime food source.

21. The latest research tells us that genetics is not as important in producing trophy racks as we once believed. The most important factor contributing to a buck's antler size is time. A given buck produces his biggest antlers during his fourth through his sixth years of life. But according to research conducted by Penn State University deer biologists, hunting pressure results in fewer than 4 percent of all bucks ever living long enough to see their third birthday.

Biologists now tell us that genetics is not the crucial element in a buck's ability to grow massive racks such as this one. The most important factor is time.

22. The trails used by mature bucks are difficult to find because they're primarily used by animals traveling alone. *Tip:* First find a major deer trail used by large numbers of does and their offspring, then scour the terrain 40 to 50 yards on either side of that trail. Mature bucks commonly use trails that travel parallel to and downwind of trails used by doe-family units.

23. Universally, the single most important advice veteran trophy hunters have to offer is this: "You have to be willing to let the younger bucks pass."

24. Surveys of successful trophy hunters have revealed that the best type of feeding area for taking a big buck is one that offers soft mast. Examples of soft mast are persimmons, wild grapes and cherries, honey locust, prickly pear, pawpaws, mushrooms, berries, and orchard fruits. The reason is not just that these foods are palatable and energy producing. As a buck ages, his teeth become worn down to the gumline, making it difficult for

Boone & Crockett Club scorers will tell you that taking a big buck like this means letting the smaller bucks pass.

The Whitetail Deer Hunter's Almanac

him to masticate hard mast (such as acorns) and woody browse (such as branch tips).

25. A solid rule of thumb is that while older deer have the largest racks, they also have the toughest venison. After you've taken your trophy and are considering meal preparation, consider only those cookbook recipes that involve tenderizing cooking methods such as marinating, braising, pressure-cooking, stewing, Crock-Potting, and the making of burger and various types of sausage.

26. Young bucks don't yet have a fully ingrained spook factor, but mature bucks are seldom fooled twice. If a big deer sees you on stand, or smells you, or hears you, or if you shoot and miss, forget about that stand producing a second chance at that particular deer for the remainder of the season. Relocate it at least 200 yards away.

27. In the deer woods, prime locations for rubbing trees and making scrapes are at a premium. Because of this, mature bucks frequently rub the same trees year after year, and create scrapes beneath the same overhanging tree limbs as the season before. When you scout, then, always begin by checking the locations of last year's sign to see if brand-new sign has been created there.

28. One type of terrain that consistently produces large racks is a wide river bottom that stretches for miles. Such areas are perpetually damp, enabling the vegetation there to better extract minerals from the soil. These nutrients are in turn passed along to bucks that eat there, allowing them to achieve their maximum antler-growth potential.

29. Biologists tell us that the number one cropland food favored by deer is the soybean. Deer first eat the seedpods, then munch the plant stems, then paw the ground to get at the roots. Some smaller soybean fields end up looking as if they've been run over by a lawn mower.

30. Radio-tracking studies in the Southeast have shown that the type of security most favored by big bucks is not thick cover but the inner recesses of deep swamps with standing water at least 1 foot deep. These are the animals' daytime seclusion spots. They bed on small dry hummocks and come out only under the cover of darkness to feed in nearby fields.

31. The world's two largest nontypical, record-book bucks were found dead, presumably of natural causes. This has prompted scientists to speculate that some bucks are such masters of evasion that they're simply unkillable by any legal means.

32. The key to finding a big buck's bedding area is first finding a doe-family bedding area recognizable by numerous, various-sized ovals in the snow or matted grass. Once you've found such a spot, search nearby high ground downwind for a larger, single bed. Mature bucks like to bed relatively close to doe-family units, which make ideal sentries.

33. What weather conditions are the most conducive to big-buck movements? Wildlife biologists say mature bucks are most active when the barometric pressure is between 29.80 and 30.29, the wind velocity is less than 10 miles an hour and coming from the south or southwest, there's a relative humidity of less than 60 percent, and there's a new moon.

34. How far a mature breeding buck will travel during the rut depends upon just one thing: the doe population. In regions where does number fewer than five per square mile, an amorous male may string his scrape line out over 7 miles or more. Conversely, in regions where does number as many as 30

How far trophy bucks travel during the rut, and how far they'll string out their scrape lines, depends upon the number of does available. If does are plentiful, a buck may spend the entire rut in a small area. If does are few and widespread, he will run himself ragged traveling many miles a day.

per square mile, a buck may travel no farther than several hundred yards on a given day.

35. There's a consensus among veteran trophy hunters that the best strategy for taking a big buck after the season has been open for several days is to forget about hunting scrapes and feeding areas. Mature bucks are now in an escape mode, so the best stand hunting strategy is setting up in a funnel (a narrow travel corridor connecting two large forested areas). The deer are continually on the move to evade hunting pressure.

36. Scientists studying the locations where trophy bucks rub tell us that 26 percent are found along deer trails, 10 percent are along the edges of logging roads, 15 percent are along streambanks, and 49 percent are randomly scattered around field perimeters and in forested areas.

37. Whether or not your region experiences a second rut usually depends on the doe population. If there are fewer than five does per square mile, there's no second rut because all the females will be successfully impregnated. If there are more than 15 does per square mile, however, many of them will not be bred and will come back into estrus 28 days later. And if there are more than 30 does per square mile, a third rut will commence 28 days after the second rut is over.

38. In cold to moderate temperatures, bucks and does of all ages usually require about 1 gallon of water per day. In hot weather,

In hot weather, smaller deer require 1 gallon of water per day and can usually find it in random puddles. But mature bucks of greater body weight require as much as 3 gallons of water per day and are attracted to ponds, streams, and rivers.

the water-intake requirement of smaller bucks and does jumps to about 2 gallons but, due to their larger body sizes, mature bucks require 3 or more gallons per day. This makes water sources, particularly ponds and streams, hot spots for hunting trophy bucks. Smaller deer, on the other hand, can generally get all the water they need from random trickles and puddles.

39. Late in the winter, does and young bucks may be active at almost any time during the day. In contrast, mature breeding bucks are now experiencing a dramatic hormonal change as their once high testosterone level crashes. This results in a change in their circadian rhythm, causing them to be most active between 11 A.M. and 3 P.M.

40. Early in the season, mature bucks eager to get on with breeding deposit priming pheromones on the trees they've rubbed. These pheromones, from the forehead glands, have the effect of chemically inducing does into an earlier-than-usual estrus while simultaneously suppressing the testosterone levels of young bucks to reduce their competition for breeding privileges.

41. Researchers have determined that mature deer (bucks and does alike) have three peak drinking times per day: 7 A.M., 11 A.M., and 6 P.M. In cold to moderate temperatures, these drinking sessions may last only minutes, but in hot weather they may span much longer time frames. These drinking times have nothing to do with thirst but are tied to daily body metabolisms and related cud-chewing periods.

42. When a number of mature bucks share the same home turf, the does often determine which bucks get to breed the most. When they visit scrapes made by the various bucks, does are able to use the vomeronasal organ in the roof of the mouth to smell and chemically analyze each buck's urine. A buck that is metabolizing carbohydrates and excreting them in his urine is healthy and virile, while a buck that is metabolizing fat and protein is beginning to decline in health and probably has a low sperm count.

43. While mature, trophy bucks are far warier than younger deer, their vision is no better. Still, it doesn't need to be: Deer eyes possess 1,000 times more motion-receptor rods than the eyes of humans. Because of this, never make even the slightest movement when a big buck is looking in your direction.

44. Mature bucks occasionally flag when they flee from danger, but this behavior is far more common among does; their waving white tails allow their offspring to easily follow them through dense, dark cover. *Tip:* If you jump a group of deer and can't immediately see antlers because of the cover, focus your attention on the animal that's *not* flagging. More than likely, that's the buck.

45. Unlike younger deer, trophy bucks entering their bedding area commonly climb to slightly higher ground and reverse their line of travel for a short distance before lying down. This enables them to watch their backtrail. When you follow tracks, always be on the alert to movements to your immediate right or left (whichever is higher ground). That's where you're most likely to see your buck, not straight ahead.

46. Mature bucks prefer to make antler rubs on aromatic trees such as cedar, pine, spruce, shining sumac, dogwood, and sassafras. They instinctively know that the oily cambiums of these species retain their forehead-gland scent longer, even during inclement weather. Conversely, immature bucks commonly rub tag alders and other saplings that have nonresinous cambiums. *Tip:* Learn which rubs not to consider when you scout for a trophy buck's whereabouts.

47. Mature bucks sometimes share scrapes; biologists are not certain why, but believe the behavior may play some kind of role in their social system. If your partner kills a trophy buck over a given scrape, check back in coming days to see if that scrape has been revisited and freshened. If it has, get on that stand double quick!

48. Veteran trophy hunters play the confidence game. If all sign indicates the presence of a big buck in an area but you don't see him after many days of sitting on stand, don't become discouraged. He may step into view at any minute.

CHAPTER 5

45 Rut Hunting Tips

Deer hunting's most exciting season is highlighted by rapid changes in the animals' behavior. Keep these important points in mind.

1. Hunting experts and biologists tell hunters not to get overly excited by finding a few scrapes during the rut. Yes, this gives your scouting a start, but radio-telemetry studies have revealed that a single mature buck makes as many as three dozen scrapes each year. So keep searching; if you've found only a handful of scrapes, you haven't scouted long or hard enough.

2. Using a rutting scent prior to the prebreeding "chase phase" isn't natural and will only spook the animals. Pay close attention to your timing, and use such scents only when the rut is clearly under way.

3. As a rule, the larger the diameter of a rubbed tree, the larger the buck that made the rub. Big bucks occasionally rub small saplings, but young bucks rarely rub large trees.

4. Scientists who conduct radio-tracking studies have learned that each mature buck makes an average of 250 rubs per year. Video

Mature bucks make an average of 35 scrapes a year, most of them from 24 to 36 inches in diameter.

recordings have shown that each rub is completed in a surprisingly short period of time—on average, less than 15 seconds.

5. The scrape of a mature buck averages 24 to 36 inches in diameter and takes approximately 15 seconds to make.

6. Rubbed trees are not indications of a buck attempting to remove the velvet from his antlers. They are visual and olfactory signposts that a buck uses to proclaim his presence and communicate information about his social ranking to other bucks and does in the area.

Antler rubs on trees are signposts that convey information to other deer. A buck usually creates a rub in less than 15 seconds; aromatic tree species such as conifers are preferred.

Don't confuse turkey scratchings for scrapes. Positive identification of a scrape involves spotting tracks and deer pellets in the pawed area, along with an overhanging tree branch that has been chewed and mutilated by the deer's antlers.

7. Biologists don't have a clear explanation for the phenomenon, but the quantity and quality of the acorn drop affects how many antler rubs bucks make each year. When there are fewer acorns than usual, there will be fewer rubs, so finding only a few rubs in a particular year doesn't necessarily mean that few bucks are around. Scout the acorn drop before you give up on a particular area.

8. Don't confuse turkey scratchings or ovals of bare soil for scrapes. A scrape will always be accompanied by a low, overhanging branch that has been raked, chewed, and broken. And there will undoubtedly be a fresh hoofprint, and perhaps even several deer pellets, in the scrape itself.

9. When you're setting up a stand so you can watch a scrape, don't get too close or a returning buck is very likely to detect you. Since bucks commonly scent-check their scrapes from 30 to 40 yards downwind, the spot for your tree stand should be 50 to 60 yards downwind of the scrape if you're a bowhunter, and farther still if you're a firearm hunter. Then the returning buck should pass right between you and the scrape with his attention focused in the direction opposite you.

10. Don't pay much attention to scrapes and rubs made around field perimeters bordering woodlands. Most of this rutting sign is made and revisited only after dark.

A buck works a scrape. Actively tended scrapes around field perimeters are revisited mostly after dark.

11. You can scout for scrapes just prior to the rut far more quickly if you simply avoid terrain with a slope factor of more than 10 degrees. The vast majority of scrapes are found on relatively flat ground.

12. When you're scouting, never touch a scrape, licking branch, or rubbed tree with your bare hands or clothing. Even the tiniest amount of human scent transferred to the sign will alert deer to your presence and cancel the sign's significance.

13. In regions where does far outnumber bucks, not all does are impregnated during their first estrus. Those that have not been bred will come back into heat 28 days later, causing a second rut to begin. In regions of severe buck-doe imbalances, there may even be a third rut.

14. The earliest rutting seasons are in the Far North. In Canada and border states such as Maine or Michigan, rutting action may begin in late October. In the Deep South, it may not begin until mid-January. In Latin America, whitetails randomly breed year-round, even in spring and summer.

15. The rut is triggered when a decreasing amount of daily sunlight passes through the eyes of deer. This reduction of light stimulates the pineal gland, which in turn sends messages to the pituitary gland to increase testosterone levels in bucks and progesterone levels in does.

In the Far North, the rutting season begins as early as mid-October. In the Deep South, it may not begin until January. This Texas buck was taken a few days after New Year's Day.

16. Bucks are capable of breeding whenever they have hard antlers, which is a five-month time span. But does are capable of breeding only when in estrus—a 26-hour time span. So in reality, it's the does that "go into rut," not the bucks.

17. When does are in estrus, it's virtually impossible to call in a buck with a grunt tube. Use a doe bleater or fawn call to call in

When a buck is tending a doe in estrus, it's virtually impossible to call him away from her with rattling antlers or a grunt tube. Use a doe call instead. If she comes to you, the buck is sure to follow.

Always rattle antlers from high ground; mature bucks seldom travel downhill to respond to rattling.

does instead. Any responding does that are in heat will have bucks trailing behind them, right to your stand.

18. When you rattle antlers, don't rattle too loudly at first. Just tickle the tines to make click-clicking sounds that simulate the sparring of immature bucks. If you start off loud and aggressive, you may intimidate and scare away bucks.

19. Immediately after the rut, exhausted bucks go into a recuperative phase lasting three to five days. Since they won't move far from their beds, now's the time to stage drives. After their resting period, bucks begin feeding in an almost nonstop attempt to regain lost body weight before the winter sets in. That's the time to hunt feeding areas.

20. If you can't find much buck sign, find the does instead. They'll attract bucks as soon as they begin coming into estrus. Where are the does? Close to the major food sources.

21. If you see a buck responding to your rutting scent by tilting his head back and curling his upper lip, he likes your scent and is trying to find the source of it. But if he lowers his head and sticks his tongue out of the side of his mouth, your scent is spooking him; try a different lure the next time you're hunting that area.

22. If a doe comes by your stand with her tail extended straight back, freeze! She's at the peak of her estrus and is signaling to a following buck that she's ready to breed.

If a doe comes by your stand with her tail extended straight back, it's a sure tip that she's ready to breed and is giving a buck trailing her the go-ahead signal. Don't move. You'll have your shot very shortly.

23. Spotting a doe still being accompanied by her most recent off-spring tells you the rut has not yet begun. When does begin coming into heat, they chase their young ones away and travel alone.

24. Don't hunt buck trails during the peak of the rut. Hunt doe trails instead, because bucks engage in trail transference—checking every doe trail in the area for indications of estrus does that have recently passed by.

25. How do you recognize a doe trail? Study the tracks in muddy areas, looking for medium-large imprints along with very small imprints, indicating does followed by offspring.

During the rut, bucks abandon their own trails and follow doe trails to monitor the breeding stages of local females. A doe trail is easily identified by its combination of small- and medium-sized tracks, which indicate a mother being followed by her most recent offspring.

26. The most intense action during any region's well-defined rutting period occurs when there is a 10°to 20°F drop in the temperature. Conversely, rutting action slows dramatically when the temperature suddenly rises far above the norm. This is not to be confused with the rut-regulating influence of sunlight; it's a separate, year-round phenomenon. Deer are always more active in cool weather, becoming lethargic when the temperature rises above the norm.

27. If you see a doe bedded in a relatively open area during the rut, freeze! Don't take your attention off her or the surrounding cover. Shortly after does are bred, they lie down to relieve pressure on their cervix and uterus. Bucks are aware of this and often wait nearby. When the doe eventually stands, a buck will rush to her side and attempt to breed her again. Scrutinize the cover and you may see him lurking about.

28. Biologists tell us that the types of places where bucks most frequently make scrapes are, in descending order of importance: field edges, ridge crests, terraced hillside benches, narrow bottomland flats adjacent to creeks, and old logging roads.

29. During the rut, bucks have been known to travel as far as 7 miles per day and as little as 300 yards per day. It all depends upon how many does are available to a buck in a given region.

30. When you're rattling antlers, simulate the sounds of a genuine buck fight by stomping the ground with your boots and raking the antlers through brush.

In regions where doe populations are very high, not all females are bred during the first rut. They'll recycle into a second estrus 28 days later, with bucks pursuing them as before.

If a nearby buck tilts his head back and curls his upper lip, he's pleased with the scent that you're using.

31. There's growing evidence that a dark-moon phase during the rut sees more intense mating behavior than a full-moon phase.

32. Never place a rutting scent on your person. A buck investigating the scent will try to find its source, and having it on you increases the chance that he'll detect your presence and spook. It's better to place the scent on low-growing brush or vegetation at least 30 yards away from your stand.

33. When you're scouting scrapes, you're most likely to encounter the buck that's working the area where you find scrape clusters. These are places where there are as many as a dozen scrapes in close proximity to each other, usually within an area no larger than an acre. The buck is more likely to revisit a cluster than a lone scrape.

34. Many experts agree that hunting a scrape area is more likely to result in success if you use a portable, climbing stand that you carry in and out each time you visit. If you use either a fixed-position stand with screw-in tree steps or a ladder stand and leave it in place, a buck visiting the area during your absence is likely to see or smell the stand and avoid it from then on.

35. If you're hunting a scrape area and either spook a mature buck or shoot at one and miss, it's unlikely that he'll give you a second chance in the days or weeks to come. Better to relocate your stand to another scrape area at least 300 yards away.

36. Try to remember where you've jumped bedded does in the past. As the rut is about to get under way, bucks will begin patrolling downwind of these bedding areas, waiting for the first does to come into estrus.

37. To make a mock scrape more effective, don't simply dribble doe-in-heat scent onto the ground; it will quickly evaporate, especially in dry or windy weather. Use a drip regulator attached to a high branch to dispense the scent one drop at a time for 24-hour periods. Replenish the scent in the regulator each time you leave your stand.

When you create a mock scrape, don't anoint it just once with scent. Use a drip regulator to continually freshen the mating invitation; refill it each time you leave your stand.

38. If you see a young buck either tending an estrus doe or actually mating with one, consider relocating your stand. If a mature buck were monitoring the doe population in the immediate area, he'd never allow a subordinate buck to breed "his" females.

39. If you see a buck approaching a scrape cautiously and in a timid manner, with his head held low and his tail tucked between his legs, you might want to pass him up. He's exhibiting subordinate behavior that indicates the scrape he's investigating was made by another, higher-ranking buck.

40. Bucks commonly scrape in the same locations year after year. They may even lay down scrapes beneath the exact tree branches and rub the very same saplings as the year before. When scouting, be sure to check the scrape and rub locations you hunted the previous year. You may even find yourself being able to use the same exact tree for a stand as you did last year.

41. If you want to take full advantage of the rut, become a bowhunter. Most state firearms seasons don't begin until after the rut is concluded, to allow for a maximum number of does to be bred before the buck population is cropped off. Bowhunting seasons, on the other hand, usually coincide with the rut period in most states.

42. Ignore so-called estrus-response scrapes. These are small in size and commonly found in open fields and meadows. They're simply places where an estrus doe has urinated and a buck in his random travels has detected the scent and briefly pawed the ground. The buck may never return to that spot again.

43. If the scrape you're hunting begins to dry out and is slowly becoming covered by windblown leaves and forest duff, it's no longer being visited and freshened by the buck that originally made it. Scout elsewhere for a hot scrape that's being regularly tended.

44. When you're scouting, take a topographic map or aerial photo and mark the location of every scrape and rub you find. When studied individually, a given scrape or rub may not seem to have that much significance. But when you look at the larger picture of many rubs and scrapes, it's often easy to discern the buck's travel pattern.

45. Severe weather ordinarily causes whitetails to lay up in cover, often for several days, until things blow over. The exception is the peak of the rut. When most of the does are in full estrus, they are very restless and continually on the move; bucks likewise are on their feet, traveling and searching for the females, regardless of what the weather is doing. So don't stay home just because high winds or driving sleet are ravaging your favorite deer woods.

CHAPTER 6

50 Stand Setup Tips

No matter what you've read, some basic tenets of tree-stand placement always hold true.

1. The most critical rule of tree-stand hunting is this: It's far more important to choose an undesirable tree in a smoking-hot location than to choose the perfect tree for your stand in a not-so-desirable spot where you're unlikely to see anything.

2. If you're hunting a farm, never carry your portable stand to its intended hang-up spot on foot unless there is no other way. There's no such thing as a walking farmer or rancher. They all drive trucks, four-wheelers, or tractors on their land, and deer become accustomed to the comings and goings of such vehicles. If you likewise ride, you'll fit right in and arouse little suspicion among deer.

Don't place a bowhunting stand in a tree directly above a scrape. Mature bucks often scent-check their scrapes from 50 yards downwind, so set up a short distance downwind to be within acceptable shooting range.

3. When you're trail watching, position your stand not along a straightaway stretch but on the inside of a bend. A deer walking the trail will be looking toward the outside of the bend and less likely to notice you.

4. If any moving parts on your stand—hinges, struts, or other attachments—begin squeaking, apply a few drops of odorless cooking oil. Don't use petroleum distillates, because their odor will spook deer.

5. Only a small percentage of tree-stand hunting accidents are the result of a hunter falling out of his stand. Most occur when the hunter is ascending or descending the tree. Wear a climbing belt (the kind utility linemen use) when you're climbing up or down your tree trunk, and a conventional safety belt when you're actually sitting in the stand.

6. If you don't like heights, use a ladder stand to get just above the second-growth ground cover so you can see better.

Ladder stands are preferred by those who don't like heights. Since such stands are no higher than 15 feet, be sure the tree you select has plenty of twisted limbs and branches to break up your outline.

The Whitetail Deer Hunter's Almanac

7. Many hunters like to position their tree stand so that they're facing the tree trunk when sitting in it. The trunk acts as a type of blind to hide behind. If you're gun hunting, the trunk offers a stable rest. But how do you draw a bow when facing the trunk? You don't. You wait until the deer has slightly passed your location; then you turn and take the quartering-away shot.

8. When you're hunting a bedding area, position your portable climbing stand so you can hunt the downwind side of the cover. If the wind direction changes on a given day, select a different stand location; if you're on the upwind side of a bedding area and a mature buck catches your scent, he'll leave and probably never return.

9. As a rule of thumb, the two-stand hunter should have one stand set up to watch a heavy-cover bedding area in the morning and another set up to watch a feeding area in the evening. Better yet, find stand setup locations on trails leading to or from bedding and feeding areas.

10. When you've found an area where you want to place a stand before the season starts, return at the time of day you plan to occupy the stand. This way you can see how the sun bathes the landscape with shadows and bright light at that time, which will enable you to select the right camo pattern to match your surroundings.

11. For maximum concealment from all directions, hang your stand in a multitrunk tree clump. A single-trunk tree standing alone won't hide your presence if a deer approaches from an unexpected direction.

12. Early in the season, don't position your stand too high; the dense foliage beneath you will obstruct your view to the ground and prevent you from getting a clear shot. Go higher later in the season, after the leaf drop.

13. If you use screw-in tree steps to gain access to a fixed-position stand, always wear gloves when climbing them. Otherwise you'll leave human scent on the steps, right at the level at which a deer's nose is operating.

14. In a hot deer-traffic area, never leave your climbing stand attached to the base of the tree trunk when you depart for home.

This stand is just a big scent bomb that will allow deer passing through the area at night to pattern you. Detach your stand from the tree and take it with you.

15. A fixed-position stand that can be folded up against the tree trunk in your absence is ideal in cold, inclement weather because it will shed snow, ice, and sleet that would otherwise encrust it. A folded-up stand is also less conspicuous to other hunters who may wander through the area.

16. Whether you're using a climbing or fixed-position stand, be sure to properly anchor it before use. Exert your body weight on the stand platform both front to back and side to side, then bounce gently. With the stand solidly anchored, it won't shift or squeak when you alternately stand and sit or reposition your feet.

17. Once your stand is mounted on the tree, use a heavy leather glove to scuff away loose bark from the trunk so it won't rub against your clothing and make noises as you climb or turn your body to get into shooting position.

18. When you use a climbing stand, the easiest and quietest way to "clean" your tree trunk as you ascend is with a small pruning saw. Stow it in your pack or attach it to a short length of rope and hang it from your stand once you're settled in.

Be flexible. If you set up and deer consistently pass far out of shooting range, don't hesitate to climb down and relocate your stand closer to the high-traffic area.

19. Always keep the term *mobile* in mind. If deer consistently walk by your stand just out of shooting range, don't hesitate to climb down and reposition your stand closer to the area they're using.

20. Try to avoid taking the same route to your stand every day; you'll eventually create a well-defined scent trail. Approach from a different direction each time, always with the wind in your favor.

21. It's easy to burn out a stand by overhunting it. Try not to occupy your stand for more than three consecutive days. Then rest it for a week.

22. The hottest big-buck stand can be ruined if you insist upon hunting from it when the wind direction is not absolutely in your favor. If the wind is coming from the wrong direction or swirling erratically, stay away. The best argument for having multiple stands in place is that you can choose the best location to hunt each day as conditions dictate.

23. To make sure you don't under- or overestimate bow-shooting distances, place markers (such as sticks pushed into the ground) at various distances around your stand for quick reference should a buck come by.

24. Once your stand is in place, have a buddy climb into it. Then walk around and look up at him from various distances. This will reveal what approaching deer will see and allow you to make necessary adjustments.

25. If you shoot at a deer and miss, or a nearby deer senses that something's wrong and runs away, consider moving your stand, even if it's only 50 yards. You must keep the element of surprise in your favor.

26. Always situate a stand so that you aren't blinded by sunlight shining directly in your face. The rising or setting sun should be at your back; that way, an approaching deer looking in your direction will have difficulty seeing you, because the bright light is in *his* eyes. This is why you'll probably need both a morning and evening stand, each facing in a different direction.

Position your stand so that when you're occupying it you'll be facing north or south. This way you won't be staring directly into bright, low-horizon sunlight at dawn and dusk.

27. Whenever you have a choice, hang your stand on the north side of a tree. Your human form will be less conspicuous, because you'll mostly be in the shade of the trunk.

28. Don't bother tying a length of thread to your bow limb to check the wind direction while you're in your stand. Due to upcurrents, downcurrents, and thermals, you want to know how the air is moving at *ground level,* where a deer's nose is, not 20 feet above the ground. A thread tied to a bush only 3 feet off the ground that you can see clearly from above is your best bet.

29. In bitter-cold weather, relocate your stands to trails overlooking the southeastern sides of sheltered black timber, such as dense cedar groves. The dark color of the trees absorbs the maximum of sunlight heat, while their southeastern sides are protected from polar blasts coming from the north and northwest. Cedars are also a favorite winter food of deer.

Every hunter should have at least one stand set up to overlook a major trail leading to a bedding area such as those often found in dense conifers.

30. When you're using a fixed-position stand, don't leave your equipment-haul rope in place during your absence. Hanging right at a deer's nose level, that rope reeks of human scent and will betray your presence in the area. Take the rope home when you leave for the day.

31 When you're hiking to your stand area, keep in mind that there may be deer beneath your stand at the very moment of your arrival. To prevent spooking them, stalk your stand. Then glass the area around your stand from 75 yards away before making your final approach. If you see deer in the vicinity, try to still-hunt them; if the cover doesn't allow for this, back off and go to a different stand that day rather than alarm them.

32. Always keep spare stand parts in your fanny pack. Nothing is more frustrating than dropping and losing a wing nut or bolt when you're beginning to mount your stand on a tree trunk.

33. Never carry a portable stand while you're scouting: You'll be tempted to commit yourself to the first good-looking spot you find. There may be a much hotter area elsewhere. Scout the entire region before making your decision, then go get your stand and take it to your chosen tree.

34. Except during the rut, deer activity usually ceases on days when the wind exceeds 12 miles an hour. Skittish because they can't effectively use their senses, the deer lay up in heavy cover. Now's an ideal opportunity to rest your hot stands, let the weather clean them of all human scent, and devote time to scouting a new region.

35. Stands with base platforms made of woven-metal grating material afford the safest footing. If your stand has a platform of aluminum crossbars or sheet plywood, accumulated sleet, ice, or snow may cause slippery and dangerous footing. You can fix this by applying sand-impregnated traction strips that have adhesive backing.

36. When one of your tree stands pays off with a big buck, spend time studying all of the cover and terrain features in the immediate area to determine why the place was so attractive to the deer. Then look for other areas that duplicate those conditions, because other big bucks might be using them.

37. Hand-carrying a portable stand through cover to the tree where you plan to mount it can be very noisy, because branches and brambles grate against the metal. Get some webbed strapping material and rig it to the stand so you can carry it on your back like a pack. This also leaves your hands free to carry other gear.

38. All commercially made stands come with a sticker that indicates their load weight limit. Don't mistake this figure as representing your body weight alone; it's the *total* safe weight the stand is designed to hold. Heavy boots and winter clothing, gun or bow, loaded fanny pack, and other gear can easily add another 30 to 50 pounds.

39. Obtain some scrap ½-inch-diameter aluminum tubing and cut it into 3-inch lengths. Next, solder these at various locations onto your stand platform and paint them flat black. When there aren't enough leafy branches around your stand to break up your outline, you can prune small branches elsewhere, carry them to your stand, and insert their ends into the handy tube holders.

40. When you're preseason scouting and picking a tree for your stand, consider what that tree will look like in coming weeks, when the leaf drop occurs. Will the now barren tree leave you fully exposed? If so, pick a different tree, one that has forks and gnarled branches to break up your body form.

41. Many successful hunters hang at least five tree stands in different locations so they'll always have a hot stand to hunt from as the season progresses and conditions change. There should be a stand overlooking a prime feeding area, one overlooking an escape trail (use it when hunting pressure mounts), one near a scraping area, one in a funnel travel corridor, and one in a stormy-weather bedding area.

42. The best time to scout for a new tree-stand location is in March or April, because vegetation has not yet grown up to hide last year's sign. Now you can also look for the shed antlers that tell of bucks that survived last season. You can even prune shooting lanes around last season's stand at this time. When opening morning finally arrives, you can then hike to your preselected tree and hang your portable stand with a minimum of disturbance.

43. If your stand seat is a canvas-sling affair or a piece of foam covered with fabric, thoroughly spray the cloth with water-repel-

Treat your canvas-sling seat with a water-repellent spray so that rain or snow doesn't soak it during your absence.

lent spray to make it shed snow and rainwater. Otherwise, when you sit down, the seat of your pants will annoyingly soak through and you'll chill out far more quickly. Or you can bring a dry thermal pad made of closed-cell foam.

44. If your climbing stand is a two-piece affair, make sure you tie a short length of rope between the upper seat assembly and the lower foot-climbing section. Otherwise, if your boots slip out of their climbing loops and the lower climbing assembly falls to the ground, you're in a fix.

45. When you're using a fixed-position stand and screw-in tree steps to gain access to it, remove the lower six steps every time you leave the stand. Take them home or stash them in nearby cover so that someone passing through the area can't steal your stand or the steps themselves. When you return, simply screw the steps back into their original holes. Another option is to secure the stand with a short length of cable or chain and a pad-

Climbing stands are two-piece affairs. Make sure a rope or strap connects the upper seat section to the lower climbing section so the lower part can't fall to the ground.

lock, although a determined thief may simply go back to his truck to fetch his bolt cutters.

46. When you scout a large tract of land for a stand site, always hunt for what's least available to the deer, because that's what will be high on their list of needs. If endless cover predominates but there are only a few widely separated food sources, the deer may bed almost anywhere but they'll be attracted every day to the places that contain food. Conversely, if food is abundant and widespread but security cover is sparse, deer can feed almost anywhere but will home in upon the cover when they want to bed or hide.

47. If you're sitting in your stand and spot a buck approaching from 100 yards away, right then is the time to slowly come to a standing position, adjust your feet as necessary, and raise your

When you spot a deer working in your direction, and he's still far out of shooting range, that's the time to slowly rise to a standing position and raise your gun or bow. Waiting until he's close invites detection.

shooting equipment. If you wait until the deer comes much closer, he's far more likely to spot your movements.

48. During the offseason, store your tree stands in a well-ventilated area that's protected from the weather. Basements and garages are poor choices because vehicle exhaust, paint, cleaning supplies, and the like will contaminate your equipment with deer-alarming odors; you'll have to thoroughly descent before the scason. Store the stands in an open-air shed or carport for best results.

49. If the best tree in a hot hunting area has a slanting trunk, make sure your stand is mounted on the side of the trunk that slants away from your back. Then if you stand to take a shot, the trunk won't tend to dangerously push you out and away from the stand. Also, when you install the stand, make any necessary adjustments so that the platform, footrest, and seat are level.

50. Stands that attach to tree trunks with chains require little annual maintenance and will last for years; just give them a quick check prior to opening day. But stands that use webbed straps or braided ropes for attachments should be carefully inspected for wear several times during the course of *each* season.

CHAPTER 7

50 Deer-Calling Suggestions

There are hundreds of deer calls on the market.
These tips will help you use them effectively.

When a deer responds, put the call down. Now let the deer hunt you.

1. Never call when a deer is looking straight in your direction. He'll surely peg your exact location and may also spot you moving. Call again only when the deer looks another way. Keep him guessing and he may eventually walk right beneath your stand.

2. Too many hunters who use grunt calls try to sound like the biggest and baddest buck in the woods. This only serves to intimidate most bucks and scare them away. If you tone down your effort so you sound like a wimp, you'll draw greater response from bucks that think they can whip you.

This doe was drifting through heavy cover when she heard a contact call and stopped.

3. If you see a distant deer respond to your call and begin coming your way, put the call down! It has performed its job; if you keep calling, you'll only increase the buck's chances of pinpointing your location.

4. An estrus-doe bleat is the perfect call to use at the peak of the rut. When a doe is in full heat, she goes looking for a buck. She periodically stops and bleats, then looks around and listens for a response from a buck. This particular call sounds almost like a standard grunt call; the difference is that it isn't continuous but includes three-second pauses between each one-second bleat.

5. When deer are slowly feeding through thick cover and can't see each other, they use a contact call to remain aware of each other's location. When you mimic this call, the key to realism is making it rise and fall in pitch.

6. If you blow your call at a distant deer, he will react almost 100 percent of the time. He may not always turn and immediately come your way, but you'll see some recognition of the call such as the deer raising his head, looking in your direction, or simply cupping an ear toward you. If none of these things happens, the buck did not hear your call, perhaps because the wind is too strong. This is a clear indication that you need to blow the call more loudly.

7. When you're on stand, pay careful attention to any deer around you. If one begins staring in a particular direction and makes a contact call, it's aware of other deer you can't yet see. Don't even blink, because a buck may be about to step into view.

8. Most call manufacturers offer cassette tapes that let you listen to how the calls are supposed to sound, and then practice before going afield. Don't worry about sounding perfect. Deer have slightly different voices, just like humans.

9. Few hunters are aware of it, but there's one type of call that's actually intended for use during drives. It's the deer whistle call, and its shrill sound will quite often cause a fast-running deer to stop dead in his tracks, giving you a moment to take a shot at a stationary animal.

10. If you prefer not to have a lot of calls hanging around your neck while you're on stand, consider one with a reversible reed that produces two different levels of volume and pitch. Or try a call

Harold Knight of Knight & Hale Game Calls using a call with a reversible reed.

with different O-ring settings within the reed, or one whose reed can be adjusted by means of an exterior push button; both types offer a wide range of volumes and pitches. For a variety of reasons, some days a particular tone works better than others.

11. When you're ready to begin your first antler-rattling sequence, don't begin too loudly or aggressively. There may be a buck nearby, and if he perceives you as a boss buck, he may run away. Better to start off rattling softly and, if nothing comes to you, gradually increase your volume and intensity.

12. More and more hunters are using the fawn bleat call to call in does during the rut. Why call does? Because a doe's maternal instinct causes her to respond to what she perceives is a fawn

in trouble. And if you call her in, any buck that's with her is sure to follow.

13. The effectiveness of a fawn bleat call depends upon its realism. If you've ever heard a fawn caught in a fence or being pulled down by a coyote, you know that it screams its lungs out. Really put on some theatrics and your call will be more effective.

14. When you're bowhunting and wearing a mesh face net, don't make the extra movement of raising the bottom of the net to place your mouth on the end of the call. Instead, simply blow right through the netting as though it wasn't even there.

15. When you bowhunt, teaming up with a partner makes calling and antler rattling doubly effective. Place the shooter in a tree stand, or in heavy cover, about 40 yards from the caller. If a deer responds, he'll usually walk right past the lead hunter to get closer to the source of the calling, providing an easy shot.

16. Is it necessary to master the use of the many different calls now being manufactured? According to a recent study conducted by biologists at the University of Georgia, whitetails make at least 15 different vocalizations. The more "deer talk" you can mimic, the more successful you'll be in your calling efforts.

17. Grunt calls used to emit only one tonal pitch at one volume level. Now many have ribbed tubes that can be extended from 4 to 8 inches to produce various pitches and degrees of loud-

Make your rattling twice as effective by teaming up with a partner.

The purpose of the ribbed tubes on most calls is twofold. By extending or collapsing the tube, you can vary the pitch. Also, since the tube is flexible, you can direct your call slightly away from yourself so you're less likely to be detected.

ness. As a rule, use the higher pitch and higher volume to get a deer's attention from far away, then reduce the pitch and volume as the deer comes closer. The higher volume is also more effective when windy weather prevents the call from carrying very far.

18. Always use a grunt-snort call in conjunction with antler rattling. Using one without the other won't re-create the actual sound that bucks make when they interact with each other during aggressive encounters.

19. Deer don't continuously vocalize among themselves, so don't overdo your calling. The exception to this rule is during the rut, when deer vocalizations of various types are far more frequent; now go ahead and call every 5 or 10 minutes throughout the course of the day.

20. Blind calling (with no animal in sight) can be effective, but calling to a deer you can see in the distance works best.

21. When you're using any kind of call, don't expect a deer to immediately turn and come your way. Quite often a deer will stare for a long period of time, trying to see the other deer before venturing closer.

22. When you rattle antlers, always pay close attention to your immediate right, left, and (especially) directly behind you. A responding buck won't come straight to you from the direction you expect, but will often circle to come in from downwind.

23. No matter how hard you fight it, the fact is that we all occasionally need to cough or clear our throat while on stand. To do this without sounding distinctly human, muffle your mouth against your jacket sleeve and try to simulate a grunt call. Then quickly follow up by blowing on a real grunt call. A nearby deer that hears your throat-clearing noise and then the genuine grunt call won't be alarmed as he would've been if you'd just coughed.

24. A predator call, such as the screaming rabbit, should be part of every deer hunter's arsenal. This was discovered by Texas coyote hunters, who found more deer responding to their rabbit calls than coyotes. Biologists believe a deer's response to a predator call is based purely upon curiosity.

25. If there's a curved, ribbed tube on the call you're using, it has a purpose. With it, you don't have to turn your body to blow your call in a different direction and thus make a movement that deer may detect. Instead, just bend the ribbed tube in the direction you want to "throw" your call. The advantage of doing this is that it reduces a deer's ability to focus upon your location.

26. Many bowhunters prefer a hands-free call to bring a deer in those last few crucial feet when they're in the process of raising the bow and drawing the string. These are short (2 inches in length) calls that are held continuously in the corner of your mouth. You can also tape the call on the wrist of the arm drawing the bowstring, so that even at full draw you can blow into the call if needed without having to relax the bowstring.

27. An alternative to cumbersome rattling antlers is a rattling bag or box. Practice with them and you'll soon be able to produce buck-fighting sounds that come close to duplicating the real thing.

28. When darkness arrives and the day's hunt is over, many hunters wonder what to do if there's a deer near their stand that won't go away. Don't simply begin climbing down, which—

A rattling box from Lohman.

predictably—will spook away the deer. Instead, bark like a dog. The deer will leave, but won't associate the commotion with human activity in the area.

29. Contrary to what most hunters think, the best time to use a grunt call and rattling antlers is not the peak of the rut. By then, nearly all bucks are paired up with estrus does. The best time to grunt and rattle antlers is right before the rut, when bucks are alone and looking for love.

The prime time to use rattling antlers or a grunt call is the three-week period before the peak. This is David Hale of Knight & Hale Game Calls.

30. If you want to grunt during the rut, use one of the new calls that allow you to both inhale and exhale. This mimics the breathless excitation of the tending grunt that bucks make when scent-trailing a doe in heat. If a buck hears this and is between does, he may respond in hopes of horning in on another buck's intended mating activity.

31. Your eyes are critical to the outcome of any calling effort. Deer have an uncanny way of slipping in close without making a sound or exposing themselves in the open. Continually scrutinize the cover in all directions around you for the slightest glimpse of a wary buck putting the sneak on you.

32. Many hunters like to saw the brow tines off their rattling antlers and use a grinding wheel to smooth down the bumps on the bases. This will prevent your hands from taking a beating when you aggressively rattle, and it doesn't affect the tonal quality of the antlers.

33. If a buck responds to your call, comes in, then detects your presence and snorts and bounds away, he's not likely to return to that location for a long time. If you want another chance at him, it's imperative that you relocate your stand at least 200 yards away.

34. During the pre-rut, be a triple threat by simultaneously using a grunt call, rattling antlers, and decoy. But for safety's sake, use this technique only during the bowhunting season.

35. Throughout the year, does are far more vocal and socially oriented than bucks. Don't be disappointed or surprised if a majority of the animals that respond to your calls are females.

36. If you call in a buck but he hangs up just out of shooting range and won't come any closer, do nothing. Stop calling and allow him to turn and walk away until he's almost out of sight. Then call. Frequently, the buck will wheel around and come racing in.

37. When you're using a grunt call, the most effective sequence is usually three brief two-second grunts with a two-second pause between each.

38. In bitter-cold weather, moisture from your breath may eventually cause the reed in any deer call to freeze. To prevent this, simply unzip your jacket a few inches and slip the call into a shirt pocket when you're not using it.

When calling, it often makes sense to just be quiet until a buck either comes in or starts to leave.

39. When you attempt to call deer, you're performing on a stage, and the more realistic you can be, the more success you'll have. This is one reason that the use of scents makes any calling effort more effective.

Antler rattling is theater at its best, so strive for realism by breaking branches, raking the ground, and stamping your feet to simulate an authentic buck fight.

40. There is no truth to the myth that large rattling antlers will call in the biggest bucks, but it is true that bleached or dried-out antlers don't yield the same authentic sounds as fresh ones.

41. If hunting pressure is usually intense in your region, you'll have your best success calling deer midweek, when fewer hunters are in the woods. Concentrate your efforts on the heaviest cover you can find.

42. When bucks are sparring in early fall, don't smash your antlers together or you'll scare them away. Just lightly tickle the antlers

Give a buck plenty of time to respond to your rattling. Some come in quickly, but others are slowpokes. Wait at least 20 minutes before moving to a new location. Murry Burnham, founder of Burnham Game Calls, took this monster.

The Whitetail Deer Hunter's Almanac

to make a sound like a flamenco dancer clicking castanets. The time to loudly clash your antlers is later during the pre-rut, when bucks are aggressively fighting.

43. If you see a buck trailing a doe and the two deer travel out of sight without responding to your call, keep calling. If the doe isn't in estrus, the buck may eventually lose interest in her and turn and come back in your direction.

44. When you're attempting to rattle in deer from ground level, don't be too anxious to leave and try another place if a buck doesn't immediately respond. Particularly on a day when there's no wind, a buck may hear your rattling from ½ mile away; it may take him 20 minutes to slowly sneak up to your position.

45. If a small buck responds to your call, don't be too anxious to take him. Wait until you're sure that he's not being followed by a much larger deer.

46. When you bowhunt, wrap your call with camo tape so that its shiny plastic housing won't create a glare in bright sunlight.

47. If there's a second rut in your area, it will peak 28 days after the peak of the first rut. About two weeks after the peak of the first rut—the pre-second-rut period—begin grunting and antler rattling again. And once the second rut is under way, resume use of your tending grunt call and fawn bleater.

48. For any call to work, deer must be able to hear it. Always concentrate your calling efforts in locations where deer are most likely to be at certain times. Early in the morning and just before dusk, call around feeding areas. In midday, call near bedding thickets. During the rut, call in the vicinity of scrapes and rub lines.

49. When you're rattling, add more realism to your antler-meshing performance by kicking gravel downhill with your boots, scuffling leaves, and breaking dry branches to simulate the various sounds that bucks make when fighting.

50. Don't expect deer to respond to your calling efforts every day. Sometimes many animals will come to your calling one day, then none the next. Only the deer can explain why this is.

8

40 Cropland Hunting Tips

Deer are where they eat. Use these cropland strategies to boost your chances of getting a farm-raised buck.

Smart hunters shun huge farms and concentrate on small, family-owned affairs whose aged equipment doesn't allow every square foot to be plowed.

1. Biologists tell us that the preferred domestic foods of deer are soybeans, corn, cabbage, melons, sugar beets, carrots, navy beans, turnips, apples, peaches, and legume grasses such as alfalfa and clover.

2. Deer normally enter croplands at the inside or outside corners, not along one of the side edges. When you're looking for a stand location, spend most of your time scouting for entrance and exit trails at these corner locations.

3. Forget about hunting huge agribusiness farms. They plow and plant every square foot, and suitable deer habitat is scarce. They also practice clean farming, in which modern equipment leaves virtually no harvest residue on the ground. Focus instead on small family farms of less than 500 acres. Here you'll find a variety of small woodlots, brushy hollows, thickets, bottomlands choked with cover, and other irregular terrain features. At harvesttime, aged equipment leaves plenty of food behind.

4. Don't overlook a harvested cornfield or other cropland just because there's snow on the ground. Deer can smell the food spillage beneath it. I've seen them paw down through a foot of the white stuff to retrieve a mere 3-inch length of broken cob.

Whitetails can easily locate spillage in cropfields by smell alone.

5. It's usually easier to obtain deer hunting permission on a farm where crops are grown than on a tract of land not used for agriculture. The reason is that too many deer can decimate certain crops and cut into a farmer's earnings; thus, many farmers welcome hunters in hopes of keeping the deer population in check.

6. It may be difficult to obtain deer hunting permission on farms just beyond the city limits sign, because these landowners are besieged by so many hunters each year. Drive a little farther into the country and you'll have much better luck.

7. Watermelons and cantaloupes are like ice cream to deer. They kick the melons apart with their pointed hooves, and then eat the sweet inner pulp. A field littered with broken melon parts is a deer hunting hot spot you should never overlook.

8. Fields of low-growing crops (grains, grasses, and truck-garden vegetables) that butt up against dense woodlots or pine plantations see the heaviest use by deer during daylight. Low-growing crops situated in wide-open areas aren't worth consideration; deer may eat here, but only after dark.

9. What's a deer's all-time favorite farmland food? Radio-tracking studies have shown that a deer will walk right through a 50-acre cornfield without pausing to reach a 5-acre soybean field. Soy-

Grains and grasses that butt up against thick cover see the most deer use, even from monster bucks like this.

beans are so highly favored by deer that they eat the entire plant: first the beans, then the leaves, then the stems. After the beans have been harvested, they'll revisit the field to paw the ground and get at the roots. If you have a choice of various types of croplands to hunt, always pick the soybean field.

Soybeans are a deer's favorite domestic food.

10. Deer are ruminants and have four-compartment stomachs; the parts are called the rumen, reticulum, omasum, and abomasum. This arrangement allows deer to feed quickly with minimal chewing, filling the first compartment. Then they retreat to bedding cover, regurgitate the cud, and more fully chew it before swallowing into the remaining stomach compartments. To eat quickly in farm country, they commonly bed close to cropland edges. In nonagricultural areas, on the other hand, they shelter far back in deep cover.

11. If there's no heavy bedding cover adjacent to a cornfield, deer commonly bed right in the corn! If hunting the perimeter edges

Hunting the edges of cornfields can often pay off.

This hunter used a portable camo blind to hunt a green field—with excellent results!

doesn't produce, stage drives. You can bet they'll be in the fields!

12. If there are no trees large enough to support a tree stand close to the cropland you plan to hunt, consider building a ground blind. Also, don't overlook the possibility of hiding behind or even inside aged equipment that's often abandoned around cropland perimeters. I once took a fine buck while sitting in the cab of a rusted, old combine. The equipment had over the years become an accepted part of the landscape, and deer that passed my "stand" never even looked in my direction.

13. Wait until after harvesttime to hunt croplands where root crops were grown. Deer seldom dig for carrots, turnips, sugar beets, potatoes, onions, or the like, but they'll eagerly devour broken pieces of these vegetables that are turned up to the surface by mechanized equipment.

14. If numerous farms border each other, try to gain hunting permission on the farm where something different is being grown. Deer are varietal feeders, meaning that their body metabolisms don't function properly on just one type of food. Therefore, if most of the farms in a given township are planted to corn and hay meadows, the lone farm that has leafy vegetables (lettuce, cabbage) will act as a magnet to the local deer population. If most of the farmers in a particular region raise orchard fruits,

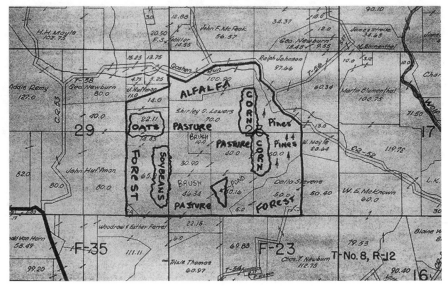

You can mark county plat maps with the locations of the crops, pastures, and forest, so you can better plan your hunting strategy.

the lone farm planted to grain (wheat, oats, sorghum) will be high on the deer hit list.

15. When hunting any cropland, try to stay on stand as long as possible each day. Deer living there are accustomed to having close encounters with vehicles, farm equipment, and farm workers, so they're not nearly as nocturnal as in nonfarm country (where they retreat for deep bedding cover as soon as the morning sun clears the horizon).

16. County plat maps, available at the courthouse at the county seat, are invaluable aids in acquiring hunting permission. They show all county and township roads, waterways, the dimensions of all parcels of land, the acreage and, most important, each landowner's name.

17. Biologists have revealed that whitetails focus their attention on soybean and cornfield spillage and remaining orchard fruits during bitter-cold weather. The reason is that the animals instinctively know these particular food types yield the highest conversion rate (conversion is the metabolic transformation of food into energy, body warmth, and accumulated fat stores). Therefore, do your research, because the farms you elect to

In winter, deer focus upon high-carbohydrate foods such as corn to help generate body heat.

hunt during the beginning of the hunting season may not be your best choices toward the end of the season.

18. During the rut, heed the old axiom: "Find the does and you'll find the bucks." The does will be found in the vicinity of whatever crop happens to be in its prime, depending on the latitude at which you're hunting and the timing of the rut in that region.

19. To thwart diseases and insects, farmers customarily rotate their crops each year by planting certain foods in different locations and, in some cases, planting entirely different foods. In other words, don't assume the cornfield edge where you took a splendid buck this year will produce another buck next year. Next year the farmer may plant oats instead of corn, or he may not plant at all—leaving that particular field to rest in a fallow state.

20. When you know deer are feeding in a certain cropland, don't install your stand right on the perimeter edge. Instead, put it on an entrance trail at least 50 yards back into the adjacent woodland cover. Does and small bucks may enter a cropland well before dusk, but mature bucks commonly stage back within the cover until full dark.

When rainfall is sparse, deer often go to alfalfa and clover meadows, where they lick dew from the grass.

21. After you've acquired permission to hunt on a farm that's rais-ing crops, ask the landowner where he sees deer feeding, where they come out of surrounding woodlands, and how they travel back and forth across the property. He lives there year-round, probably seeing deer almost every day, and his insights can greatly reduce your scouting time.

22. You've placed a stand overlooking a low-growing cropland such as an alfalfa meadow, grain field, or soybean field. When you go to your stand in the predawn darkness, don't hike across the open cropland; you'll likely bump deer off the food and send them running. Instead, circle widely and approach your stand by coming through adjacent woodland cover. Con-versely, for the evening watch, don't hike through the wood-lands to reach your stand, because you'll likely spook deer from their beds; take the shortest route right across the open cropland.

23. Although grass legumes such as alfalfa and clover are deer mag-nets, their attraction is strongest in the early fall when they're still lush and green. Later in the fall and into early winter, after several hard frosts, the grasses go into dormancy, become dry and woody, and are no longer as palatable or nutritious.

24. In warmer, southern climes where certain crops are grown well into the fall and early winter, ask your farmer host about the specific dates he intends to apply fertilizer, lime, insecticide, and anhydrous ammonia. These treatments leave a residual bitter taste on the food, and deer will feed elsewhere until a heavy rain or two washes the chemicals off the plants and into the soil.

25. During periods of drought, the hot spot for deer hunting is a legume meadow, and the prime time to be on stand is early morning. The reason is that deer will spend almost all of the nighttime hours in the meadow, alternately bedding in it, feeding, and licking dew from the grass. As soon as the morning sun burns off the dew, they'll retreat into nearby shaded woodland cover.

26. When you're hunting a cropland, never be so anxious that you settle for a low-percentage shot at a deer standing at a poor angle. Unlike deep-woods deer, which often have some destination in mind and may pass by your stand rather quickly, cropland deer come to feed. This means they dawdle around, nibbling on this and that, allowing you to patiently wait for a perfect, high-percentage shot.

27. When you're scouting for sign of deer feeding in croplands, examine the food to make sure you're not fooled by the presence of other critters dining there. When you find cornstalks knocked to the ground and only the tender tips of the ears have been bitten off, it's the work of raccoons, opossums, or turkeys, not deer; deer nibble randomly upon the entire ear and don't have to knock the stalk down. When you find legume grasses, grain stalks, or soybeans sheared off cleanly, it's the work of rabbits, squirrels, or armadillos; deer have a rough-textured grinding pad on the upper surface of the mouth, and grains and grasses on which they have foraged have a torn, ragged appearance.

28. When you're sitting on stand and a doe steps out of woodland cover into a cropland and repeatedly looks back over her shoulder, freeze! She may be keeping tabs on her fawns trailing behind, but she may also be looking at a buck following her, especially if the rut is in progress.

29. There are many different types of corn. The unanimous favorite of deer is sweet corn, but during the fall and winter hunting

months this is found only in the Deep South. North of the Mason Dixon line, so-called field or stock corn is what deer utilize most. If you find a cornfield in which the ears seem smaller than usual and the stalks are only 4 feet tall, avoid it. This is popcorn; it becomes hard and brittle during its curing process and is rarely eaten by deer.

30. If you and your partners hunt a farm and have a friendly relationship with the landowner, he'll probably be willing to sell you a small part of his crop and leave it standing to attract more deer than harvested spillage otherwise would. Two or three rows of corn adjacent to a forested edge, a ½-acre portion of a soybean field, or ½-acre of root crops that are turned to the surface but not collected is sufficient to attract deer throughout the hunting season.

31. Although farmlands generally have high whitetail populations, you can't take shortcuts when it comes to scouting. Because agricultural regions have such abundant supplies of food, and because the animals' cover-use and travel options are so varied, more scouting is actually necessary than when you're hunting a region where cover and food are scarce and the animals are therefore more predictable. Be a year-round whitetail scout in farm country.

32. When you're stillhunting through a cornfield, don't make your way down the long rows—deer will spot you from afar and quickly slip away. Instead, hunt perpendicularly to the rows. Poke your head through the cornstalks, look right and left down the row, quietly step into that row, then look into the next row, and so on.

33. When you scout a cropland for deer entrance and exit trails, keep in mind that most of them will be in the vicinity of the corner or perimeter edge that borders the thickest cover in the area.

34. An easy preseason way to discover which crops on a farm are being visited by big bucks is to go there in the late afternoon. Simply park several hundred yards away, preferably where there's a vantage point overlooking one or more crops, and, using binoculars, spend some time scanning the areas thoroughly. One or two sessions at each cropland will allow you to quickly assess the deer population and how the animals are approaching the food source.

35. Most farm families have dogs, and they commonly allow their pets to freely roam about the property. If you're sitting on stand and hear dogs barking in the distance, or actually see them traveling past your stand location, don't assume that they've chased all of the deer out of the county and ruined your hunting. Farmland deer become quite accustomed to sharing their habitat with dogs, and even livestock that's being woods-pastured. Deer don't seem to perceive these animals as a serious threat, just a common annoyance. I once watched an old mule chase four does out of a rye pasture; when the mule eventually walked back to the barn, the deer quickly returned to the rye to resume feeding.

36. If you're hunting with several partners, ATVs and trucks can be used to drop off and pick up hunters right at their stand sites. This practice seldom alarms farmland deer, because they're accustomed to seeing vehicles. But if you want to remain in the farmer's good graces, never drive across a hay meadow or through any other planted crop; stay on established equipment trails.

37. Many farms that raise crops also have at least a few head of livestock, and that means fenced pastures. This situation creates many types of additional stand-location possibilities, especially in places where a crop butts up against a pasture. Low places in a fence where deer jump over, or slight depressions beneath fences where deer crawl under, may indicate regularly used trails; look for tracks and hair on the wire. Gates that are periodically left open for more than a week at a time—as stock is rotated from one pasture to another—are another option.

38. Never overlook the possibility of an interior-cropland blind, especially in low-growing crops such as legume grasses, soybeans, or truck-garden vegetables. Quite often there will be a low place in the middle of a field that's always damp or even soupy. Farmers give these places a wide berth when plowing and planting so their equipment won't get stuck. Conversely, the center may also contain a large, high pile of rocks that were picked from the field over the years. In both cases, if weeds have grown up to afford concealment, you've got a natural blind in place from which you can cover the entire cropland.

Never overlook orchards, as even big bucks like this can't resist the fruits. Use a cover scent when hunting.

39. When you're using a cover scent, always select one that allows you to blend with your surroundings. Near an orchard, slice an apple in half and rub the exposed sides on your clothing. Many vegetables, such as cabbage and broccoli, are highly aromatic; collect a few leaves, crush them in your hands, and then rub your palms on your jacket sleeves and pant legs. Farmers commonly plant pines in various areas to serve as crop-protecting windbreaks. Snip off a few small sprigs and put them in your pockets; put others in your clothing-storage bag. On unused land adjacent to crops, you may find crab apple trees and other wild species that can be used to make you fit in. Also, if a pasture borders the cropland you're hunting, step in a cow patty so the cow scent on your boot soles covers your human scent as you walk to your stand.

40. There is no scientific explanation for it, but immediately after snow cover melts, two of the first crop foods that deer home in on are winter wheat and oats. If it's cold and snowy today, but a thaw is predicted for tomorrow and you know of a wheat or oat field, be there!

CHAPTER 9

50 Tips for Using Camouflage

Learning how to disappear into your surroundings gives you a decided edge on game.

1. Many camo and hunting accessory companies sell pin-on leaf clusters. Put them on your hat and coveralls to achieve a realistic three-dimensional appearance. You might also consider using textured, loose-leaf camo garments. Both prevent deer from focusing on a solid human form.

2. Scientists have confirmed that deer can see and are spooked by ultraviolet light. When you buy camo, look for a hang tag that says "no UV brighteners." If the garment doesn't have this tag, spray the clothing with a blocking agent such as U.V. Killer, made by Atsko/Sno-Seal and available through most mail-order hunting catalogs.

3. How many different camo outfits do you need? Most experts have at least six. You should have three different color patterns to match changing foliage as the season wears on, and three different weights to accommodate mild, chilly, and bitter-cold temperatures. Depending upon where you live and hunt, a snow-camo outfit may also be called for.

This composite photo shows how we perceive camo (the upper half) and how deer perceive the same garment because of their ability to see ultraviolet light (the bottom half). Buy camo that contains no ultraviolet brighteners or treat the garment with a UV block.

Owning just one camo outfit isn't enough. You should own different outfits to blend in with different types of terrain and cover, in a wide range of weather conditions.

4. Don't be a cheapskate. When your camo pattern begins to fade after several years of use and many washings, it's no longer doing its job. Retire it to lawn and garden work and buy new duds.

5. When you use greasepaint, close your eyes and daub a bit onto your eyelids. Otherwise, every blink will look like the flash of white semaphore flags.

6. Never use pure white garments for hunting in snow; you'll stand out as the brightest thing in the woods. Even in full sunlight, snow has a muted dirty-white or grayish cast due to overhead clouds and tree shadows. Counter this by buying a snow-camo outfit with brown or black zigzags to simulate brush or branches.

7. If your stand platform is made of solid plywood, paint the bottom blue with dark gray streaks, so a deer looking up will see what he thinks is sky through tree branches. On both sunny and overcast days, the two contrasting colors will help your stand blend in better than it would if it had a solid, unpainted finish.

The object of all our efforts. A whitetail's eyes, nose, and ears are its primary defense mechanisms. When an animal puts them into use simultaneously, it's a wonder hunters ever score.

Morning's first light on opening day is what a deer hunter's dreams are made of.

Strive for realism in your target practice. You can't eat straw bales with bull's-eyes on them.

It's all really very simple. Deer are where they eat, so find the food and you'll find the deer.

Two bucks sparring in the preseason. Come the rut, they'll know who's who in the local pecking order.

Ray McIntyre, president of Warren & Sweat Tree Stands, is one of the country's foremost acorn experts. He likes to surprise hunters by telling them there are 34 species of oak trees east of the Mississippi.

Rubs on saplings are not indications of where a buck has removed his antler velvet. They're scented communication signposts, created to pass along information to other deer in the area.

Getting ready while filled with anticipation is a ritual as old as time.

Whitetails are exciting to hunt, but sometimes they're fascinating just to watch.

The hallmark strategy of veteran deer hunters is: "Walk a little, watch a lot."

Map out a game plan. Topographic maps and aerial photos are among a hunter's most valuable tools.

Three of the greatest hunting innovations of the century are superior-quality camouflage, the grunt tube, and the compound bow. (Photo courtesy Realtree Outdoors)

Mature whitetail bucks are creatures of superlatives. Graceful. Cunning. Elusive. And purely wild.

Still waiting in hopes of seeing something, and still convinced that an unsuccessful day afield is better than a good day at the office.

When pressured, whitetails use favored escape routes to evade danger. Set up near such escape trails, and you'll have a good chance of seeing a buck—especially on opening day.

Preseason scouting is the name of the game. Perennially successful hunters often have their buck picked out well before opening day arrives.

Does are every bit as intriguing as bucks. Smart hunters know that if you want to get a buck, it pays to find the does.

Stand hunting is a matter of reverse geometric progression. If sign indicates the presence of deer, the longer you wait without seeing anything, the better your chances become. (Photo courtesy Realtree Outdoors)

A hunter glassing on a foggy morning, early in the season. Fog, drizzle, and light snow are all perfect conditions for stillhunting.

The eyes say it all: focused attention and determination.

Success! Dragging a deer is both hard work and a labor of love.

Deer hunting is no longer strictly a guy thing as every year millions of women also take to the field.

Harold Knight, of Knight & Hale Game Calls, with a splendid Kentucky buck.

Will Primos, of Primos Game Calls, with a Mississippi whitetail he called into bow range.

Like fingerprints, deer antlers are unique. This buck was aptly named Tall Tines.

Whitetails are catalysts for a hunting tradition across the country, bringing together family and friends for an annual rite each fall.

Neither cold nor snow can thwart a dedicated hunter's determination.

Shed antlers in the snow: This buck will be around next season, if a hunter is lucky enough to find him.

8. When you're applying greasepaint, take care to cover those facial areas where perspiration makes your skin shine, such as the bridge of your nose, cheekbones, forehead, upper lip, and chin.

9. Use flat-black spray paint to cover stand-mounting chains, braided wire cables, and padlocks that otherwise may shine in bright sunlight.

10. Attach cut leafy branches to your stand to break up both its appearance and that of your legs.

11. Never put a stand on a ridgeline where you'll appear as a silhouette against the horizon. Just below the ridgeline is much better.

12. Use a felt-tipped pen with indelible black ink to cover shiny garment buttons, zipper tabs, belt buckles, and bootlace grommets.

Pick a tree found with plenty of background cover to help break up your silhouette.

13. Don't wear shiny jewelry that may reflect light and spook deer. Leave wristwatches, ID bracelets, necklaces, and earrings at home.

14. If you use a fixed-position stand and either screw-in tree steps, hang-on tree steps, or climbing sticks, install them on the opposite side of the tree from the direction you expect deer to approach. Otherwise, an approaching deer may see them, become suspicious, look up, and detect your presence.

15. When you use a ground blind made from natural materials, design it so you can shoot around one of the sides rather than over the top. Otherwise, you'll expose yourself like a jack-in-the-box.

16. Use a camo face paint that also contains an insect repellent and is made from an odorless cold-cream base that easily washes off. Several brands are available through mail-order hunting catalogs.

17. If you're dark or olive skinned, you still need to apply grease-paint or your skin will shine when you perspire. But instead of using dark paints, use a combination of tan and light green.

18. As a safety precaution, firearm hunters are required to wear varying quantities of orange. But you can remain visible to

Author's son with a monster whitetail. Wearing camo with fluorescent orange helped him stay hidden.

other hunters and at the same time lessen your visibility to deer by wearing camo or other blocky clothing patterns elsewhere on your body.

19. Mix and match. Sometimes, given your stand setup, it's smart to wear a different camo pattern on your upper torso than on the lower part of your body. A leaf pattern on your jacket and a tree-trunk or branch pattern on your trousers can in some instances really help you blend into your surroundings.

20. Most tree stands these days are factory-painted in drab colors, but some aren't. Never use a brand-new, shiny aluminum stand right out of the box. Spray-paint it with a mottled design in flat brown, flat black, and olive-drab.

21. A camo-cloth gun sock on your firearm will prevent its shiny barrel and stock from glaring in bright sunlight. Camo gun tape is also available, but most hunters don't like what it sometimes does to the finish on a firearm's stock.

22. If you have blond or shiny black hair, wear a head net beneath your hat to conceal your locks.

23. If your stand is hung in an area bathed in bright sunlight, even your slightest movements will be magnified out of proportion. Much better to hang your stand in a place where there will be shadows during those times you plan to be in it.

24. If you can afford only one camo outfit, buy one that has a combination of tan, brown, and black, because these colors will blend with the widest variety of cover and terrain. Get it in a lightweight fabric for mild weather but a size large enough that you can layer insulating garments underneath in cold weather.

25. When on stand, your hands move more than any other part of your body. Never forget to camouflage them, with either paint or camo gloves.

26. When you apply greasepaint to your hands or face, your goal isn't a solid, uniform coverage. Instead, create a combination of various dark-colored splotches, irregular bars, and zigzags, leaving a bit of light-colored skin showing through here and there.

Don't simply put on a camo suit and think you're ready to hunt. To disappear in plain sight, it's also necessary to use camo on your face and hands (note the difference between the gloved and ungloved hands).

27. When you're selecting a tree for your stand, anticipate the eventual leaf drop and pick a tree that will retain its foliage longer than other species. Oaks and poplars retain their leaves deep into the winter, and conifers have needled branches year-round.

Choose your camo based on the types of trees near your stand.

Wear a camo pattern that matches the leaves of your chosen tree.

28. Trees that look like stark-naked telephone poles are poor stand choices. For your camo effort to work, you must be able to blend in with something such as deeply grooved bark, branches, forked limbs, or leaves.

29. If you take binoculars into your tree stand, don't point them toward the sun. The glare from their lenses can alert deer.

30. Even in very light breezes, deer cover is continually in motion, swaying back and forth. This means you can move, too, but only in ultraslow motion, in time with the breeze. This way deer won't single out your movements as different from everything else.

31. Avoid finely detailed camo patterns. Intricate twig and leaf patterns—especially if they're uniformly dark in color—may at close range appear realistic. But as seen by deer at a distance,

Visual disruption is what makes camo work. Large, blocky patterns accomplish this much better than small, detailed patterns.

these overly busy patterns will blur out and silhouette you as a blob. Large, bold camo patterns and contrasting colors do a better job of breaking up your human form.

32. If you stand hunt at midday in an area bathed in bright sunlight, pick a tree with a dense overhead canopy of leaves. Otherwise, you might cast a human shadow on the ground that can spook close-in deer.

33. Your camouflage is less visible to approaching deer when natural cover is behind rather than in front of you.

34. When you select a tree for a stand you'll use during the firearms season, always consider the direction a deer is most likely to approach from, and where the sun will be at that time. If you look through a scope when you're directly facing the sun, it can be impossible to see your target, and the glare off the scope lens can make you conspicuous.

35. Visual disruption is the key to disappearing in plain sight. To create it, make sure you have leaf and tree-branch cover at the level of your stand, even if this means hanging the unit slightly higher or lower than you'd prefer.

36. To achieve a 3-D appearance, incorporate texture into your camo effort whenever possible. Strips of burlap sewn or pinned to your camo outfit work wonders, as do small tree branches inserted between the struts of your stand.

37. If camo is overdone, it will actually make you *more* conspicuous. In thin cover, for example, deer will pick you off in an instant if you and your stand look like a botany project gone awry. Study your surroundings and try to match them.

38. Once you've chosen a tree for your stand and are in full camo, tell your hunting partner the general area in which you'll be and ask him to try to find you. If he has a hard time doing so, you've done your job.

39. While in your stand, in full camo, have your hunting partner walk around nearby and look up at you from different directions. He may spot areas you've overlooked that need camo attention.

40. Considering tonal value is important when you're attempting to match the cover you'll be hunting in. *Tonal value* refers to the

degree of brightness that a fabric color emits. If you're wearing a light green camo pattern but are hunting in dark green vegetation, for example, you'll stand out like a snowflake in a coal bin.

41. In bitter-cold weather, when greasepaint or a head net doesn't protect your face from the cold, consider wearing a contoured camo face mask made of hard-pressed fabric to block the wind.

42. If you've found the perfect tree for a stand, but it has no limbs or leafy branches to break up your outline, create your own cover. Before the season opens, prune several bushy branches at some other location, pull them up into your stand with a haul rope, then nail them in place around your stand.

43. Rub your rattling antlers with a dark mahogany stain. The motion of ivory-colored antlers being clashed together vigorously can be spotted by deer from a long distance away.

44. If you take a thermos bottle up into your stand, make sure it's wrapped with camo duct tape to hide any stainless-steel or other shiny parts.

45. It might sound silly, but wearing drab-colored socks is important to total camouflage. When you sit down on your stand seat, your pant legs tend to ride up a bit. When moved, white or

A wary buck can spot you using ivory-colored rattling antlers from a long distance.

light-colored socks that are exposed above your boot tops may catch a nearby deer's eye.

46. When you prepare a ground blind before the season, take your camo coveralls and prop them up with a stick behind the finished blind. Then walk off varying distances, turn around, and look back at your blind. You'll see exactly what an approaching deer will see, and this may reveal certain aspects of the blind that need more attention.

47. Many bowhunters wear knee-length rubber boots to keep their scent to a minimum, but neoprene has a shine to it that may cause a glare in bright sunlight and reveal your presence. Before putting them on, rub your boots with steel wool to dull the shine.

48. After a season's use, the paint on the rungs of ladder stands often become worn down to shiny metal. Be sure to touch them up with a drab-colored spray paint before the next season.

49. Many hunters like the age-old trick of using a burned cork to darken their faces. It's inexpensive and works fine in cold weather. In hot weather, however, perspiration trickling down your face can create white streaks, thus defeating your camo effort.

50. Some hunters become careless on stand during predawn darkness and just as the final minutes of evening dusk are settling in. They reposition their feet, stretch tired muscles, or alternately stand up and sit back down again, thinking that the reduced light level is making their movements less conspicuous. The opposite is the case, however, because unlike humans, deer can see just as well in total darkness as in daylight.

10

41 Ways to Improve Your Deer Drives

When deer aren't moving, sometimes the only way to fill your tag is to force them into action.

A drive master should know the terrain and the travel direction deer are likely to take.

1. Always appoint a drive master or captain to be in charge of your group. He doesn't have to be the most skilled hunter, but he should have the best knowledge of the terrain, where deer bed, and where they usually go when pushed.

2. Putting on a drive with a large group of hunters can be time consuming and difficult to organize. Smaller groups of three to six hunters are easier to organize and move around.

3. Driving huge tracts of woodland cover takes an eternity and affords deer too many escape options. If I'm given the choice

To keep logistics under control, try to keep the number of hunters in a drive party to six.

between driving two 100-acre tracts of cover and driving twenty 10-acre tracts, I'll take the smaller drives every time.

4. When you're driving cover, if there's a big buck in there with numerous other deer, as a rule he's either the first one to come out, or he won't come out at all.

5. When you drive cover surrounded by open terrain such as low-growing crops, pastureland, prairie, or fallow fields, always use flankers. These are drivers who work noisily along the outer edges of the cover, preventing deer from spurting out along the sides and bolting across open ground.

6. Immature pine plantations, with individual trees no more than 8 feet high and packed tightly together, can hold amazing numbers of bedded deer. The thick whorls of branches close to the ground limit visibility to mere feet and give deer a feeling of great security.

7. Whenever possible, place stand hunters on higher ground than the cover to be driven. If the cover is thick, they'll be able to look down into it and see deer sneaking ahead of the drivers. Also, any shots they take will be vertical, into the ground, rather than horizontal and through the cover being driven.

8. When you're planning a drive and considering the wind direction, remember that it's better to allow the deer to smell the drivers than the hunters placed on stand. The best situation of all is driving in a crosswind, as the deer won't be able to catch the scent of either the standers or the drivers.

9. Shots presented during drives are nearly always at moving animals. Therefore, the best scopes for firearms are the wide-angle variety with relatively low, variable-power magnification. A perfect example is a wide-angle 2.5 x 5X, which allows you to quickly find your target in the lens.

10. As drivers move through cover, they should try to maintain a straight line so that no one gets too far ahead or too far behind the others. Since a member of a drive line may also get a shot, two rules must never be violated: All hunters on the drive line must wear fluorescent orange, and no hunter on the drive line should ever take a shot to his immediate right or left. Shots straight ahead are acceptable if the stand-hunters are far in the distance or on high ground, such as steep hillsides overlooking a bottomland being driven.

It's best to engineer your drive so the deer catch the drivers' scent, rather than that of the standers.

11. Drivers should always be alert to what's going on behind them. Quite often a bedded buck will remain bedded, allow the drivers to walk past him, then get up and flee. At other times, if the cover is especially thick, deer may succeed in sneaking back through the drive line.

12. If you're convinced that there's a big buck in a patch of cover but your first drive didn't push him out, drive the cover a second time from a different direction.

Mature bucks are notorious for their ability to circle and sneak around drivers. If you're sure there's a big buck in the cover but he doesn't come out during the drive, drive the cover again, this time from a different direction.

13. Consider occasionally using a fishhook drive if you're having problems with deer doubling back. In this maneuver, the drive line progresses through the thick cover in the usual manner. Two-thirds of the way through the drive, however, two drivers reverse their line of travel and slowly sneak hunt back in the

The fishhook involves two hunters backtracking halfway through the drive.

opposite direction. Quite often they'll get point-blank shots at deer that are focusing their attention on the drivers moving away in the distance.

14. Many bowhunters prefer to use a recurve bow for drives. It's light in weight, and it can be drawn more quickly and shot more instinctively than a compound bow with sight pins.

15. An aerial photo is invaluable to a drive party hunting a tract of land for the first time. With an aerial photo, the drive master can give the drivers a firsthand look at the cover they'll be penetrating and point out any changes of direction they'll have to make. Likewise, he can visually show the stand hunters where to situate themselves and where they can expect to see deer.

16. Try a backstanding drive to bushwhack any bucks that try to sneak through the drive line. A backstanding drive line progresses through the cover in the usual way, hoping to push deer to standers positioned ahead. But in this case, a couple of stand hunters are placed behind the drivers at the spot where the drive line initially enters the cover. These hunters often get action about halfway through the drive.

17. Don't discount tiny pieces of isolated cover. Especially after hunting pressure has been on for several days, a brushy culvert or thick patch of undergrowth only 1 acre in size may hold a good-sized buck.

18. If a member of a drive party shoots and kills a deer partway through the maneuver, don't suspend the drive right there; there may be more animals in the immediate area. Tie a 2-foot length of orange ribbon on a branch near the fallen deer's location. Then resume the drive. The downed animal can be removed from the field after the drive is completed.

19. If you only have a few hunters available for a drive, make one without standers in position. This is called the line drive and it's perfectly suited to rectangular-shaped plots of cover surrounded by open ground. The drivers line up and simply begin sneaking through the cover. Deer jumped ahead often travel parallel to the face of the drive line, because they know that if they flee directly away they'll eventually reach the end of the cover and have to expose themselves by crossing open ground.

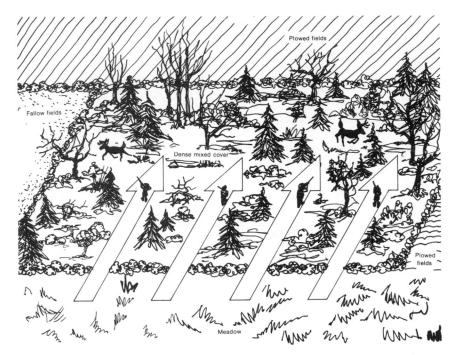

The line drive is perfect for situations when there aren't enough hunters to both drive and stand.

20. Driving a cornfield is ideal for bowhunters, and the type of drive you should use is called the diagonal shift. No hunters need be placed on stand. The drive members space themselves 50 yards apart along one edge of the cornfield. Beginning at one end of the drive line, the first hunter steps into a row, looks right or left, then steps into another row. After he's gone through about 10 rows, the next hunter on the drive line enters the field. In this manner, the drive line moves diagonally through the field, causing deer to circulate. Shots can safely be taken to the right or left, down the rows, without endangering the staggered line of hunters.

21. It might seem that making a bowhunting drive in a cornfield would be impossibly difficult because the shooting lanes are so narrow. If you make the drive on a windy day, though, the wind hits the cornstalks and ricochets in random directions. The deer may hear you and smell you, but since they can't pinpoint your location they lock up and hold tight, offering a shot to the next hunter to step into that particular row.

The two-man drive is ideal for smaller patches of cover.

22. Make sure standers and drivers all have wristwatches that are perfectly synchronized. Otherwise, if the drivers begin entering the cover even five minutes too soon, before the standers have had time to get into position, all is for naught.

23. Even two hunters can stage a drive. One enters the cover and begins slowly stillhunting. The other hunter waits 15 minutes and then enters the cover, taking the same route as his partner, who is now several hundred yards ahead. A deer that detects the lead hunter will often make a circle to get behind him and offer a shot to the trailer.

24. If the cover is exceedingly thick, the drivers should be spaced closely enough that they can see each other. As the cover opens up, they can spread out a bit. Since undulating terrain may cause even close drivers to lose sight of each other, each hunter should have a crow call to occasionally inform the others of his location.

25. The windiest days, with gusts exceeding 15 miles an hour, are the best ones for making drives. Deer won't be moving naturally anyway, and the sounds and visual effects of wind—

not to mention swirling air currents carrying scents in random directions—confuse the senses of driven deer, causing them to travel slowly and cautiously and therefore present easier shots.

26. Hunters designated as standers should sneak hunt as quietly as possible to their assigned positions. If they move too fast or are too noisy, they may spook deer and send them hightailing in unintended directions.

27. Excellent drives that limit a deer's travel options are those in which one or more sides of the cover have large, natural barriers that are difficult to cross. Examples include sheer unclimbable rock walls, wide rivers, and lakeshores.

28. Just because you drove a piece of cover one day and didn't push out any deer doesn't mean you shouldn't return to drive the same cover the next day. Deer may have moved into the area during the night.

29. Many hunting parties wait until the final days of the season to stage drives. But typically, the hunting party that fills the most tags makes drives exclusively, beginning on opening morning. If you prefer to participate in drives rather than to stand hunt, team up with other hunters who also prefer drives.

30. When you're making many drives during the course of a day, take your aerial photo or topographic map afield with you. You and everyone in your party now have an instant, visual reminder of how the drives are to be conducted. Otherwise, some drivers or standers may forget the instructions given back in camp.

31. A map or photo taken afield for reference should first be sprayed with a waterproof document sealer, available in any art store. This will make it durable for field use and protect it from the elements.

32. Once a stander has reached his assigned location, it is imperative that he not move. Yes, while he's waiting, he may eventually see a slightly better vantage point only 50 yards away, but he should trust the drive master's knowledge of the terrain and how deer escape through it. Also, the drive may already have begun. Deer may already be headed in his direction, and any movements may reveal his presence.

33. If you've already filled your tag but your partners haven't and they prefer to wait on stand, ask if you can help them out by

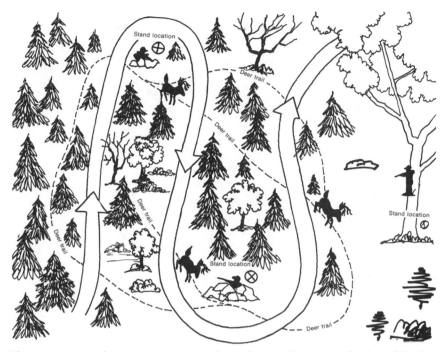

The one-man drive comes into play when a hunter who has filled his tag wants to help his partners on stand by keeping the deer circulating through the area.

making solo drives. Don't make any effort to be sneaky. Just hike around the terrain as though you're a forester doing a tree survey or a farmer counting livestock. Deer won't spook, but they will move to let you pass and, in so doing, may walk by one of your partners on stand.

34. Is there one type of drive situation that's better than all others? Yes! It's a long, cover-choked ravine that at some location bottlenecks down into a narrow passage or funnel that escaping deer must squeeze through to gain access to distant areas.

35. If you've obtained permission to hunt a farm but no one in your group is familiar with the terrain, that leaves you without a drive master to organize each maneuver. Or does it? No! Talk with the farmer or landowner, who probably sees deer every day. He can suggest how to drive the various cover formations and where to place standers. Better yet, invite him to participate in the drives with you.

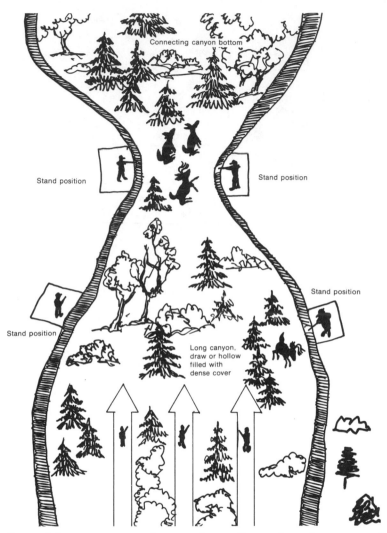

The funnel drive can give the members of your hunting group the best chance at getting a deer.

36. If you're a driver, don't walk right by large brush piles, blowdown tree crowns, or jackstrawed logs without kicking them a few times with your boots. A deer may be hiding right in the middle, waiting for you to pass. Kicking his hideout is likely to put him on his feet.

37. If your hunting grounds are large, consisting of several-thousand-acre tracts of real estate, study your topo map or

A big whitetail buck moves along, pushed toward standers by quietly moving drivers.

aerial photo and divide it up into smaller segments that can be driven more intensively. This will also reduce the escape options available to any bucks in the area.

38. Loud, raucous pincer movements with the drivers whistling and shouting make it difficult for the stand hunters to score, because the deer usually panic and come racing by too quickly for them to make accurate shots. This is especially the case when the stand hunters are using archery equipment. Silent drives, on the other hand, gently push the animals in predetermined directions, with the deer slowly sneaking off and offering better targets.

39. First-time deer hunters, or those unfamiliar with the terrain to be driven, should initially be designated as standers. Let them gain experience with the way each drive is carried out before they're assigned to be drivers in days to come.

40. Drive-party members should agree upon a universal signal in case it's ever necessary to temporarily or permanently suspend a particular drive that's under way. Unexpected things sometimes happen, and a shrill blast on a whistle will inform

everyone involved that the drive is no longer in progress and the group should return to the starting point.

41. If you're a stander and see deer racing in your direction, but they're moving too fast through thick cover for a sure shot, make a loud noise such as a screaming-fawn bleat or even a whistle. Chances are that the buck that's about to run by you will briefly slam to a halt to determine what's going on, giving you precious seconds to center your sights on him.

11

50 Effective Ways to Use Deer Scents

Fool a deer's nose with these all-time best tidbits of advice.

There are countless deer scents on the market. More important than the brand is using a given scent in its proper context.

1. Always use scents in their proper context. For example, use a doe-in-heat scent only during the rut; at other times of year, when the animals aren't mating, it'll probably confuse or even alarm the deer you're hunting.

2. To make a deer scent last longer and remain at full strength, don't dribble it onto the ground. Instead, saturate a wad of cotton with it in a film canister. To use, lift it out like a wick; to

Place your scent in a film canister for longer lasting results.

store, simply push it back down and replace the lid. Never touch the cotton with your bare fingers. Use a stick.

3. When you're bathing, use an odor-free soap—one that contains no perfume, lanolin, or cold cream, because these have odors deer can detect. pHisoDerm is reputed to be the best; it's available in any pharmacy, and is used in hospitals to cleanse surgery patients of odor-producing bacteria.

4. Food scents (such as apple, acorn, or grape) are not specifically intended to attract deer by convincing them that something

A territorial infringement lure drew this buck into range.

The Whitetail Deer Hunter's Almanac

good to eat is nearby. These are masking agents that hide human odor and should be used only in their rightful places. For example, use an apple scent when you're hunting in or around an orchard.

5. A territorial infringement lure should be used only during the rut and only in regions where buck populations are low. This scent is designed to both attract and enrage a resident buck by simulating the presence of a nonresident deer intruding upon his turf.

6. If you see a deer lower his head and stick his tongue out of the side of his mouth, your scent is spooking him. Next time, use less of it or try something else.

7. Odor-neutralizing sprays are popular, but read the label to see if your chosen brand can be applied directly to your skin. If not, use an odor-neutralizing powder. If you run out of either, baking soda is a good substitute.

8. It does no good to bathe with a scent-free soap and then dry yourself with a towel washed in a scented detergent and placed in a dryer with a scented fabric softener.

9. The areas of the body that produce the most odor-producing bacteria are the groin, underarms, feet, sternum, and small of the back. Keep several scent-free, moistened towelettes in your fanny pack and give yourself a quick sponge bath whenever necessary. They're also handy for cleaning up after you field-dress a deer.

Use an odor-neutralizing spray to help keep yourself scent-free.

10. The largest excretory organ of the body is the lungs. Each time you exhale, you breathe out millions of molecules of distinctly human odor. Try not to eat odor-producing foods that cause bad breath when you're hunting.

11. If you're a bowhunter, consider wearing knee-length rubber boots with your pant legs tucked in. Unlike leather boots, rubber boots don't hold human-related odors and transfer them to the ground when you hike to your stand.

12. Take advantage of natural scents whenever possible. When you're hunting near a pasture, step in a cow patty as you hike to your stand. Near a swamp, briefly step in the black muck. Near an orchard, slice a fruit in half and wipe the pulp onto your clothes. In a pine thicket, crush a handful of pine needles in your hands and rub the oil onto your clothing; if your hands are sticky, rub them with a bit of dirt.

13. When there are numerous deer trails coursing through your area and you can watch only one, use a trail-block scent to divert deer toward the area that your stand overlooks.

14. After laundering your clothes in a scent-free detergent, hang them outside to air-dry and remain free of household odors.

15. To remain scent-free, don't put on your boots and outer garments and then drive to your hunting area. It's better to stow them in a plastic bag, drive to your hunting spot, then dress on location before heading to your stand.

Trail-block scents are alarming to deer. When strategically placed, they will cause deer to leave blocked trails and take the one you're watching.

Always launder your hunting garments in a scent-free detergent.

16. Interdigital scent is released from between a deer's hooves and deposited on the ground as the animal walks, to communicate the deer's gender and travel direction to other deer. This is one of the most popular scents to use on your boot soles when you hike to your stand, because it not only helps cover your own scent but may also encourage a deer to follow the scent trail to your location.

17. Don't try to economize by saving leftover scent from one year to the next. When the season is over, throw it away; buy fresh scent that's at full strength next year. Although some hunters freeze leftover scent, others believe this practice changes its composition.

18. If you see a deer tilting his head back and curling his upper lip, he's exhibiting the Flehman response, named for the biologist who first identified it. This behavior indicates that the deer is smelling an odor he enjoys and would like to find its source.

19. Only masking scents designed to hide human odor should be placed on your person or at your immediate stand site. Place all other lures at least 30 yards from your stand, to prevent deer from pinpointing your exact location.

20. After taking a buck, many hunters remove the tarsal glands and tie them to their boots as a natural cover scent. The glands can be placed in plastic bags and frozen for future use.

Don't use attractor scents—only masking scents—once you're in your stand.

21. Odor-neutralizing sprays should be applied only to your exterior clothing and boots, not to your skin. With some people, or some products, direct skin application may cause a rash or allergic reaction.

22. Odor-neutralizing powders are intended for use on bare skin, to both make you scent-free and absorb moisture, which is the precursor of odor-producing bacteria.

23. When hunting in or around conifers, place sprigs of pine needles in your pockets to provide you with a natural cover scent. Pin one to your cap to help you blend in with your environment.

24. For a natural cover scent, fill a small sock with deer pellets, tie the neck closed with string, and tie the tag end to your boot to drag while you stillhunt.

25. When you've finished preparing your stand location and are hiking out, your final task is pruning occasional trailside branches and stalks of vegetation that you'd otherwise have to push aside. This prevents contaminating the cover with your scent.

26. When you're field-dressing a deer, tie off the bladder's urethra in the usual manner. Then, before you cut the bladder free, untie the string and fill a plastic bottle with the deer's urine by exerting gentle pressure on the bladder. Many hunters insist that

this is the best cover scent to place around the stand, especially during the rut.

27. If there are several scrapes in the immediate area but you can't cover them all from your stand, cancel all of the scrapes but one and then hunt it. Kicking leaves into the scrapes you don't intend to hunt doesn't work, because wind drift commonly causes leaves to fall into scrapes, and bucks merely reopen them. The surest way to cancel a scrape is to cut and discard the overhead licking branch.

28. When you thoroughly descent yourself before a hunt, avoid using any personal hygiene products that reek of perfume. Examples include shampoo, toothpaste (brush your teeth with baking soda dissolved in water), aftershave lotion, deodorant, cologne, hair tonic, mouthwash, bath talc, and foot powder.

29. If you use screw-in tree steps, thoroughly spray each step with an odor neutralizer after installing them. Then, whenever you climb the tree to occupy your stand, wear gloves rather than touching the steps with your bare hands.

30. When you drive to your intended hunting location, don't put your portable stand in your car trunk or pickup bed before stowing it in a large plastic bag. With some stands, the extra-large size—a leaf and garden bag—may be required. Otherwise, your stand is sure to pick up odors that deer can detect.

31. There is no logic to thoroughly descenting yourself and then trekking afield carrying a firearm that reeks of a petroleum-based gun oil. This type of oil is fine for off-season storage, but it makes sense to remove it for hunting. Use a degreasing solvent and relubricate the firearm with an odorless oil. Don't try to economize by using vegetable cooking oil; it begins to solidify when the temperature falls and may impair your firearm's function.

32. If certain parts of your portable stand begin squeaking, don't use a petroleum-based oil. Instead, apply the same odorless oil that you used on your firearm. In the case of stands, vegetable cooking oil *can* be used, because stands don't have moving components with wafer-thin tolerances.

33. If you have to change a flat tire or otherwise repair your vehicle while en route to your hunting location, forget about hunting

that morning; you'll smell like you just finished an eight-hour shift at the vulcanizing plant, and you'll spook the big buck you've so carefully patterned. Go home and repeat your thorough descenting regimen in anticipation of the evening hunt.

34. Even if you use a scent in its proper context, it may alarm deer in the area. For example, a given brand of pine scent that's derived from the oil of white pine may spook deer in a plantation of red pines, jack pines, or other conifer species. Always read the bottle's label or instructions to match your scent as closely as possible to the cover you'll be hunting.

35. Animal-based cover scents such as fox or coyote urine can do a wonderful job of masking human odor, but only if those species are indigenous to the region you're hunting. If they're not, all you'll do is draw attention to your location.

36. Deer hunters commonly wash most of their hunting garments in scent-free detergents. But what about garments made of wool or insulated with a high-tech fiber that need to be dry-cleaned, and then come back reeking of dry-cleaning solvent? Many of these garments can be washed at home as well, with specialized products such as Woolite (available in most grocery stores) or Sport-Wash (available through most mail-order hunting catalogs).

This bowhunter used a red fox urine scent to camouflage his human scent.

37. No matter what you eat, deer can still detect breath odor at close range. You can substantially reduce the concentrated odor molecules in your exhaled air by occasionally chewing unflavored chlorophyll or alfalfa tablets (available in any pharmacy), plain Clorets gum, or even a sprig of parsley.

38. If you hunt in a region where the wind commonly reverses direction or swirls unpredictably, placing a deer scent somewhere nearby may be ineffective. Instead, completely encircle your stand location with 8 or 10 scent bombs (saturated cotton in film canisters). No matter which way the wind blows, you'll always have scent working for you.

39. If your bowhunting shooting alleys through thick cover are so narrow that a walking deer can pass entirely through one with a single step, now's the time to use a shock scent. This means using a scent out of context, such as an apple scent in a region where there are no apples, or a doe-in-estrus scent during the nonmating period. Place the scent in the shooting alley; when a deer detects it, he'll slam to a halt. He'll bolt soon, but not before offering you a precious few seconds to make your shot.

40. Many hunters are convinced that insect repellent spooks deer. If insects drive you buggy, you can significantly reduce your dis-

Detecting a scent that's uncommon for the area, this buck has frozen in his tracks—giving you the split-second you need to take the shot.

comfort by wearing lightweight gloves and a head net. This is a common practice among bowhunters, but firearm hunters should heed the advice as well. Or consider an odor-free insect repellent; several varieties are available through mail-order hunting catalogs.

41. To obtain the maximum benefit from odorless bath soaps, start using them a week or two before the season opens. Not only will your skin and hair become as odor-free as possible, but you'll leave little human scent in the woodlands when you work on your preseason scouting and stand-site preparation.

42. Few serious deer hunters use fuel hand warmers in cold weather, because the burning fluid or fuel sticks make you smell like a kerosene lamp. Switch to odorless, chemically activated heat packs. These are inexpensive and come in assorted sizes; each generally lasts about six hours.

43. There's a never-ending debate as to whether human urine alarms deer, but why take the chance? Carry a plastic bottle with a tight-fitting lid in your day pack.

44. When you bathe, do so in the morning just before you leave home or camp for the day's hunt. If you bathe the night before, your body will have had a full eight hours to farm a new crop of skin bacteria, and you'll be exuding strong human odor long before the day's hunt is over.

45. If you save buck tarsal glands, one way to extend their use without having to freeze them is to soak them in a pint-sized bottle containing glycerine (available from any pharmacy). In two days, the glycerine will have absorbed the glands' musky pheromones. The syrupy liquid can then be transferred to a smaller bottle and used afield in the same manner as any other (bottled) tarsal scent.

46. Deer commonly follow a scent trail to its concentrated source. If you apply scent to your boot soles and hike a long distance to your stand, then, the "concentrated source" will be where you parked your vehicle and first applied the scent, not at your stand! The correct procedure is to apply a little scent as you leave your vehicle, then periodically stop while hiking to apply more.

47. When stand hunting, many bow and gun hunters tie a thread to the upper limb of their bow or gun barrel to continually moni-

As you hike to your stand, stop every 100 yards and add more scent to your boot pads. The scent can lead bucks right to the area you're watching.

tor the direction of the wind. But cover and terrain contours may cause the wind direction to be slightly different at ground level than it is 20 feet up a tree. Use the thread gambit, but also tie a second thread from a branch near ground level for the most accurate information.

48. When you scout for deer sign, never touch it with your bare hands. A returning animal will quickly become aware of your presence.

49. When you're applying scent to tree trunks or branches, place it about 4 feet off the ground. That's the level at which a deer's nose primarily operates.

Most scents will carry for longer distances if they're placed off the ground so they're better exposed to breezes.

50. Deer scents are not a panacea. They can never single-handedly ensure success. Look at scents as aids that can tilt the odds in your favor—*after* you've tapped your reservoir of woodsman-ship skills and knowledge of deer behavior.

12

50 Bitter-Cold Hunting Tips

To get a deer when it's cold out, learn how to stay warm, realize that deer behavior changes when the temperature falls, and score with these all-time best cold-weather hunting tips.

1. Instead of taking a thermos bottle of hot coffee or tea to your stand, take a bottle of beef or chicken broth. Coffee and tea have no nutritional value, but broth will help your internal furnace generate body heat.

2. When the temperature falls, relocate your stands. Deer need extra fuel in bitter-cold weather and will be searching for high-energy foods such as acorns, corn, winter wheat, or soybeans. Locate your stands near trails leading to sources of such foods.

3. South-facing slopes may be as much as 15°F warmer than north-facing hillsides. This is where you can expect to see the most deer activity—and you'll be more comfortable yourself.

4. Try the new chemically activated heat packs instead of hand warmers that use solid fuel sticks or liquid fuel. When they're burned, fuel sticks and liquid fuel give off an acrid, oily odor that's sure to defeat any other efforts you make to remain scent-free. Chemically activated heat packs last just as long, have no odor, and come in assorted sizes so you can put one in each boot, one in each glove, and others in various pockets.

5. When the temperature dives, your usual gun oil and lube may slow your firearm's action to a molasseslike crawl. As the coldest part of the season approaches, use a solvent spray to remove the present oil and lube, then give all moving parts a light touch of high-viscosity oil. Some hunters swear by sewing-machine oil.

6. On the coldest days, carry two pieces of thin indoor-outdoor carpeting to your stand, one 12 inches square and the other 18.

When the temperature dives, deer often congregate around mast-bearing trees or still-standing corn.

At your stand, sit on the larger piece and place the smaller one under your boots. These will act as barriers between your anatomy and the cold metal parts of your stand, keeping you amazingly warm.

7. The bushy plant staghorn sumac has a higher fat content than any other native forage. Deer instinctively know that this plant generates high levels of body heat and will begin gorging on it when the temperature falls into the single digits. The plant is easily identified by its bright red seed clusters and gnarled branches. It stands 3 to 6 feet tall and grows in thick groves on open, sunny hillsides.

8. If you have a long hike to your stand, stow your heavy outerwear in a day pack and put it on after you arrive. If you wear it while walking, you'll perspire heavily; then you'll get cold within 30 minutes of taking your stand.

9. Always have a backup ground blind or two that you can use as an alternative to your tree stand if snow, ice, or sleet are in the forecast.

10. If you're cold, the one thing you don't need is an alcoholic beverage. Alcohol's effect on your blood circulation will make you feel much colder than you really are. Better to have a hot cup of soup.

11. Aside from staghorn sumac, biologists say that the favorite native foods of deer in winter are white cedar, red maple, mountain maple, aspen, and red osier. Ask an agronomist which of these trees are prevalent in your area and how to identify them. Then hunt them hard, especially just before and after storms.

Smart hunters always have at least one ground blind ready to use as a backup.

12. When you return to camp, don't bring your shooting equipment and optics into a warm cabin or tent. Condensation, fogging, and other problems may arise. Leave your gear in your car or truck.

13. When you're determining where to place a tree stand that you know in advance will be used in cold weather, situate it so that a large portion of the trunk area protects you from the prevailing wind direction. Either that or try to have a screen of thick conifers on your upwind side.

14. Unless your doctor advises otherwise due to your personal health history, modestly increase your salt intake in cold weather. Explorer Paul Petzold of the National Outdoor Leadership School (NOLS) tells trainees that salt sends a greater blood flow to the extremities, thus keeping your hands and feet warmer.

15. When you're parking your four-wheel-drive vehicle back in camp at day's end, point it facing in the direction you'll be departing early the next morning. Leave the transmission in first gear (or neutral) and the transfer case engaged. This will allow you to start the engine and immediately drive off in the morning. Otherwise, everything may be so frozen or sluggish that you can only shift into gear after a prolonged period of engine and gearbox warm-up time.

16. Deep in the winter the circadian rhythm, or daily activity cycle, of deer changes. Now their prime activity periods are no longer dawn and dusk but midday, from 11 A.M. to 3 P.M. If it's too cold

When you return to camp at day's end, park your vehicle pointing in the direction you'll be leaving in the morning, and leave the transfer case in gear. Otherwise, a prolonged warm-up period may be required before you can shift and go.

to stay on stand all day, it might make sense to sleep in and not depart camp until 10 A.M. This ensures that you'll be hunting the peak activity period.

17. As you hike to your stand or stillhunt, try to step on patches of sun-dappled snow. These patches will be softer and offer quieter footing than crusted snow in shaded areas, which will cause you to make crunching sounds as you walk.

18. On any shooting equipment equipped with a scope, be sure to use quick-remove lens covers so that snow, sleet, and rain don't fog or splatter the glass and give you a distorted sight picture.

19. Bowhunters should consider switching from feather fletching to plastic vanes if they expect a combination of cold weather and

Bowhunter with good-sized buck he shot while stillhunting.

precipitation. Feather fletching can collect moisture, which results in erratic arrow flight.

20. Place a short strip of tape over your firearm's muzzle to prevent snow and sleet from going down the barrel. This also prevents snow and mud from getting into the barrel if you slip and fall. When the moment of truth arrives, you can shoot right through the tape with no loss of accuracy.

21. Most deer hunters know that multiple layers of garments will trap dead-air spaces and provide greater warmth than a single heavy layer will. But keep in mind that this applies not only to shirts and pants but to gloves and socks as well. Another tip is to warm your socks and gloves before a fireplace or suspend them over a lamp shade before you leave camp. Your hands and feet will stay warmer longer because of it.

22. In driving winds, look for deer to bed on lee hillsides or up against thick walls of cover.

23. Stay attuned to warming trends, which always see an increase in deer activity. If the temperature hovers around 0°F for days on end, a mere 5° upward spike will see deer on the move.

Wear multiple layers of clothing, and give special protection to your head and face.

Swamps and other low terrain can be hotbeds of deer activity.

24. Most firearm hunters agree that mittens that have liners and a slot hole for the trigger finger are much warmer than conventional gloves.

25. Swamps can be excellent places to find deer in cold weather. Since they're lower in elevation than the surrounding terrain, they're protected from the polar blasts that sweep across the higher, nearby ridges. Also, the constantly decaying organic matter in swamps and subsequent release of methane gas are chemophysical ways for the earth's crust to release heat. Such lowland, boggy areas can be as much as 15°F warmer than higher ground only a few hundred yards away.

26. Which high-tech insulating materials are the most popular among cold-weather deer hunters? Look for garments containing Chlorofibre, Damart-thermolactyl, Thermax, polypropylene, Thinsulate, DuPont Hollofil, Polar-Fleece, or Gore-Tex.

27. Don't discount the idea of hunting a recently harvested cropland just because it's covered with snow; there's sure to be spillage on the ground under the white stuff. Deer are easily able to smell the food and then paw down through a foot of snow to retrieve it. Simply hike the perimeter of the field until you find the spot where the majority of tracks enter the food source.

Bowhunters who like to shoot barehanded should consider an insulated muff to keep their hands warm.

28. Many bowhunters like to wear a glove on the hand that draws the string but hold the bow's handle barehanded. If the handle is made of laminated wood—and especially if it's made of metal—wrap it with thick moleskin. It won't feel as cold. An option is to use an insulated muff.

29. When you plan your deer-camp menu in anticipation of bitter-cold weather, go heavy on dishes that will help your body generate heat. This means meals that include large portions of pasta, beans, peas, nuts, fish, and dairy products. The fellow who has a double helping of macaroni and cheese and several glasses of milk will stay warmer the following morning than the hunter who has steak, french fries, and beer.

30. When a deer is within range, don't shoot until it presents a perfect shot angle. When it's bitter cold, deer commonly stand per-

Pasta, bean dishes, and dairy products are the best cold-weather fuels for your internal furnace.

With unspooked deer, there's no need to shoot right away. Better to wait for the ideal shot angle—such as this broadside shot.

fectly motionless for long periods of time, because too much moving around expends body energy. Be patient. Eventually the animal will take a single step forward, or turn just slightly to the right or left, and in so doing provide a better shot than he did just seconds earlier.

31. If your portable tree stand creaks every time you shift your weight, try standing and "resetting" it by bouncing lightly with your feet spread on the stand platform. If this doesn't work, reach into your pocket for the small squeeze bottle of odorless corn oil you remembered to bring and give the squeaky joint a shot.

32. If you come upon tracks on snow-covered ground and have to decide whether to follow them, don't let the presence of dew-claw imprints or drag marks mislead you into believing that the animal is a buck. Bucks and does both have dew claws, and they show whenever a deer's hooves sink into snow. Moreover, if the snow is more than a few inches deep, both sexes' hoof tips will leave drag marks.

33. Snow cover dictates the use of snow-camo, but keep in mind that a solid-white garment isn't a wise choice. Snow isn't pure

white but has a grayish cast, accentuated by irregular, dark-colored shadows cast from overhead branches. Your camo will match your surroundings if it's ivory colored with an overlay of brown, black, or gray splotches or streaks.

34. When you're stillhunting or staging drives, concentrate on thick groves of cedars. When packed tightly, cedars are preferred bedding cover for whitetails. They're also a favorite cold-weather food, and deer don't have to spend energy traveling long distances from bedding sites to feeding areas.

35. When the temperature hits rock-bottom, deer follow the sun during the day. You'll find most of them on east-facing slopes in the morning, south-facing slopes during midday, and west-facing slopes in late afternoon. Don't waste much time hunting north-facing slopes, which are the coldest and receive the least sunlight.

36. If you don't like shooting a bow with gloves on, prevent your hands from getting cold by getting an insulated hand muff that's held in place at waist level with a strap. Also buy a bow-mount bracket for your tree stand, so your bow will remain in the upright "ready" position. This way, you can remove your hands from the muff and reach for your bow with a minimum of movement.

37. If you bump a deer in cold weather and see him bound away, sit down and wait motionless for at least 15 minutes. Then begin making a slow, wide arc in hopes of intercepting him up ahead. You'll likely have a second chance at him, because deer don't run as far in cold weather as they sometimes do in cool or mild temperatures.

38. Many bowhunters like to reduce the draw weight of their bows when cold weather begins setting in. A reduction of 10 pounds will make your bow easier to draw when you're bundled up in heavy clothing and won't significantly reduce your arrow velocity or trajectory.

39. Cold weather means different things to deer, depending on where they live. The species lives as far north as latitude 52, which stretches across Manitoba and sees winter temperatures as low as −40°F. Yet what's described as "cold weather" in southern Alabama may be 30°F. Begin using your cold-weather hunting tactics, therefore, when temperatures fall significantly

A reduction in draw weight made it easier for this bowhunter to make a killing shot.

lower than the norm for that specific region. In Manitoba, deer would react to 30°F in the dead of winter as if it were a heat wave.

40. When you're tent camping without some form of heater, stuff all your clothes, including your boots, into the bottom of your sleeping bag. Your body heat will keep them warm during the night.

41. Dry coldness does not inhibit deer activity levels as much as damp cold. So if the relative humidity is higher than the norm in the region you're hunting on a given day, don't expect much natural deer movement. As a result, stand hunting is not likely to be productive. Better to stillhunt or stage drives.

42. There are numerous brands of portable heaters on the market that burn odorless, jellied corn oil. Most are intended for duck hunting and ice fishing, but some of the smaller, lightweight versions can also be placed between your feet in a ground blind or on a tree stand's base platform to keep you warm during severe cold weather.

43. If there's one time during the hunting season to use your binoculars, it's in cold weather with snow on the ground. Deer often stand motionless for long periods of time now, and their dark winter coats make them far more visible against a background of the white stuff.

44. One key to staying warm is not allowing your blood circulation to be slowed by restrictive garments. Loosen your bootlaces a bit, don't wear gloves that have elastic wristbands, and take off your belt and use suspenders to hold up your trousers. Also, when you're in your tree stand, don't allow the backs of your knee joints to press tightly against the forward edge of the seat.

45. When cold weather has been present for more than a week, water becomes critical to deer. This is especially the case when it's a dry cold and the deer are packing their bellies with dry browse such as leaves and twigs. Yet most static sources of water are frozen over now. So scout for moving water such as a stream or brook and pick a waiting spot where a trail crosses it. In time, you'll see deer coming to drink.

46. Some diehard, all-day stand hunters take a sleeping bag to their stand locations. They then step into the bag, pull it up, and tie the drawstring around their upper chest region to remain warm in the coldest weather.

47. If you wear gloves in cold weather, do what mothers often do with children's mittens: Tie a string to one glove and run it up your sleeve, across your shoulders, then down the opposite sleeve to the other glove. This way, if you momentarily take a glove off to unwrap a sandwich or shoot and drop the glove, it won't fall 20 feet to the ground.

48. Pay attention to the barometer. If it begins to drop rapidly, a storm system is approaching. Deer will soon go into thick cover to bed, but until the front actually arrives they'll be feeding heavily. A rising barometer in coming days signals the passage of the storm system, causing deer to leave their beds en masse and head to feeding areas.

49. An old but true adage is that if you want to stay warm, wear a warm hat, because the head and neck region is where most body heat escapes. Some hunters say a Russian-type fedora with earflaps, made of looped pile or animal fur, is the warmest headwear obtainable. Others prefer a fully insulated hood that covers not only the head but also the face and upper neck region.

50. If you take a deer during a period of prolonged cold weather, it's wise to skin and butcher it as soon as you get home. If you let it hang for just one day, the carcass will freeze solid and pose all kinds of problems.

In cold weather, the best line of defense is a warm hat.

13

40 Tips for Bowhunters

Taking a deer with a compound or recurve bow is, to many, the ultimate accomplishment in hunting. These tips can help you do it.

1. Because arrows outfitted with hunting broadheads often fly differently than arrows outfitted with field or target tips, it pays to practice with the same broadheads you'll be hunting with. You'll occasionally have to replace the razor-blade inserts when they become too dull for hunting use, and you may have to replace the whole broadhead if it doesn't have inserts. If economy is important, practice with field tips during summer, then switch to broadhead practice as the season gets closer.

2. When you buy a new bow, fine-tune it by shooting through a large sheet of white paper tacked to a square wooden frame.

To take bucks like this, you must spend a good deal of time prior to the season fine-tuning your equipment.

(Place straw bales behind the wooden frame to stop the arrows.) When you examine the tear holes, you can determine if your arrows are fishtailing or porpoising in flight. Ideally, you want to see a round shaft hole surrounded by perfect fletching cuts. If you're getting tail-high cuts, tail-left cuts, and so on, the remedy is to either slightly move the plunger button in or out, or adjust the arrow rest. Since every bow and each brand of arrow rest is different, consult the owner's guide for exact fine-tuning techniques.

3. Strive for the most realistic shooting practice. Shoot arrows at life-sized 3-D foam deer targets, not at straw bales with bull's-eyes. And don't simply place the deer targets out in the open; position them in shrubbery, under low-hanging tree branches, and in close proximity to other cover, to simulate actual shooting conditions.

4. The most common causes for an arrow wobbling in flight are an untuned broadhead, an untuned nock, or a bent arrow shaft. Use an inexpensive tabletop device called an Arro-Check to fix the problem. Lay the arrow on top of the device's opposing bearings and spin it rapidly. If the tip of the broadhead scribes a wide circle, replace it with a new one. Now check the nock the same way, and replace it if necessary. If the arrow still wobbles in flight, the shaft has a minor bend that the naked eye cannot

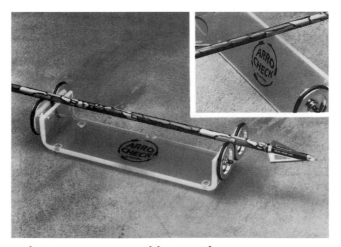

It's easy to diagnose arrow problems with an arrow spinner made for the purpose.

The Whitetail Deer Hunter's Almanac

see; either take the shaft to your pro shop, and have them straighten it, or remove the broadhead and discard the defective shaft.

5. When a deer jumps the string, he instantaneously crouches to load his leg muscles with springed tension in preparation for flight. When he does this, the arrow frequently flies over his back. He never actually sees the arrow and attempts to duck it, however. Rather, he's reacting to the sound of the bowstring being released. Since an arrow from a compound bow travels at an average of only 250 feet per second, yet sound travels at 1,088 feet per second, the noise of your bowstring reaches the deer five times faster than the arrow. Dampen your bow noise with string silencers, but also remember to aim slightly lower. To achieve the recommended lung shot, for example, the aiming point should be the heart.

6. When you engage in shooting practice, wear the same clothing you'll be wearing while actually hunting, not casual clothes. The hunting clothes will undoubtedly be heavier and bulkier, and this will slightly change the way you hold and draw your bow.

7. The cams and wheels of compound bows have an annoying habit of squeaking at precisely the wrong moment. Some hunters lubricate them with silicone spray, but this attracts dust and grit. Better to use a small pinch of graphite powder. The cable guard may also squeak upon occasion, but due to the wear of the cables on the guard, graphite powder will quickly wear off. Keep a pencil stub in your pocket and frequently blacken that part of the cable guard contacted by the cables.

8. How high should a bowhunting stand be? Let the shape of your chosen tree answer that question. If the tree looks like a straight, naked utility pole, a stand height of 25 feet or more may be in order. But if the tree has a multiple-forked trunk and many gnarled branches at a lower height—both of which will adequately break up your body outline—then hanging your stand at only 8 or 10 feet may be sufficient.

9. A bowhunter's ideal shot at a deer comes when the animal is standing broadside or quartering slightly away, which exposes the largest organ, the lungs. Don't settle for less or be too impulsive to shoot; deer tend to dawdle around, and in many cases they'll eventually offer the shot you want.

This is your shot!

10. Even with a finely tuned bow, broadheads that have replaceable razor-blade inserts with cutout vents tend to fly more accurately than broadheads with solid-surface blades; the latter often plane a bit, especially in brisk breezes, causing the hunter to miss his point of aim.

11. If you know your shot at a deer was not as accurate as you would have liked, how long should you wait before following the blood trail? The rule of thumb is half an hour if the shot was in the front half of the animal, and three hours or more if the shot was toward the rear. An exception to this rule occurs during inclement weather. Then you must take up the trail immediately, or rain or snow will quickly obliterate it and eliminate any chance for recovering the animal.

12. What's the best type of arrow fletching, turkey feathers or plastic vanes? Both have benefits and shortcomings. Turkey fletching is more forgiving when you make mistakes such as not smoothly releasing the bowstring, but in inclement weather feathers tend to become matted. Plastic vanes won't correct even a slight bit of arrow wobble, but they're immune to moisture; just bump the arrow shaft with your finger and water droplets will fall away.

Turkey feathers are more forgiving—but plastic fletching is better in inclement weather.

13. Many bowhunters hang a grunt tube and binoculars around their necks, but these can cause problems when you're attempting to draw. It makes more sense to stow these items in large cargo pockets so they don't get in the way.

14. A peep sight on your string can shift after numerous shots if it's not permanently secured in place, and this will of course destroy accuracy. Many veteran bowhunters like to tightly wrap dental floss on the string immediately above and below the sight and then liberally paint the floss winding with clear nail polish or superglue to make it durable and prevent it from unraveling.

15. Buying a hunting bow from a department store or through a mail-order catalog is beneficial only from the standpoint of getting a good price. You need more than that, and it's rare to get a bow custom-fitted to your needs through such retail outlets. That's why many serious hunters prefer to deal with a local pro

Work on your angles by shooting from an elevated vantage point such as your garage or house roof.

shop. You may pay a bit more, but the draw weight of the bow will be adjusted exactly as you want, arrows can be custom-cut in accordance with your measured draw length, a bow sight or custom arrow rest can be installed, and future tune-ups or repairs by a factory-authorized dealer are a breeze.

16. When you're shopping for a new bow at a custom archery shop, shoot several models and brands on their indoor target range (another service not offered by department stores and mail-order catalogs). High-tech compound bows are fitted with a wide variety of wheels and cams in too many designs to mention here. As a result, one bow model may draw easily and be perfect for target archery but be far too noisy and therefore unsuitable for deer hunting. Another bow's wheels may be dead quiet on the draw, but its breakover point—the point at which the draw weight suddenly lessens—may be unacceptable for your hunting purposes. You have to decide on these and other factors to satisfy your personal hunting needs, and the only way

Put a dab of fluorescent paint on your sight pins to see them better in low light.

you can do this is by actually shooting and comparing numerous bows.

17. If you'll be bowhunting from a high tree stand, don't practice across level ground. Shoot from a stand hung in a tree in your backyard, from the roof of your garage, or from some other elevated vantage to master the acute downward shooting angles. Likewise, if you'll be hunting from a ground blind, practice while kneeling or sitting on a stool.

18. If you're commonly on stand at the crack of dawn or at dusk, and have difficulty seeing your metal sight pins in the low light, switch to plastic glow pins. Or dab a bit of fluorescent paint onto each metal pin. If you use lighted sight pins, be sure to change the battery at the beginning of each season and keep a spare in your fanny pack.

19. Which is better, a cutting-tip broadhead that you must sharpen, or a chisel-point broadhead with replaceable razor blades? Cutting-tip heads penetrate easier because they begin severing hair and hide the instant the broadhead makes contact with the animal. Chisel-point broadheads, on the other hand, must push through the hair and hide before the razor blades can do their cutting work. Balance this against the fact that sharpening cutting-tip broadheads takes a good deal of time; plus, they must be sharpened often, because repeatedly pulling them out of a quiver and shooting them at targets quickly dulls them. Chisel-point broadheads need no time-consuming sharpening, though; just slip new ones in place.

20. Should your broadheads be turned in their arrow-shaft sockets until the blades are perfectly in line with the fletching? Engineers for broadhead companies say no. If by coincidence the blades end up perfectly aligned with the fletching, fine. But a less-than-perfect alignment is also fine; any effect upon arrow trajectory or flight will be so minimal that you'll never notice it.

21. Unless you practice throughout the year, it's wise to release the draw weight of your compound bow before putting it into off-season storage. Do this by making four to six turns of the limb bolts to lessen the stress on the limbs and reduce stretching of the string. Simply unstring a recurve or long bow after each day's hunt or practice session.

22. The risers and handles of compound bows are made of light-weight metal composite materials. If they come into contact with an aluminum or carbon arrow, a metallic clinking sound is created that will put nearby deer on full alert. Pad your arrow shelf, sight window, and handle with moleskin or felt that has a self-adhesive backing. The material also makes the handle warmer to hold in chilly weather.

23. Bow-tuning problems associated with erratic arrow flight can often be traced to a cheap arrow rest. It's false economy to spend $350 on a new bow and then slap on a $2 arrow rest. Check the catalog of the company that made your bow, and you'll undoubtedly find a wide array of arrow-rest options. The higher quality rest you select, the better accuracy you can expect.

24. In hot weather, never leave a long or recurve bow in an enclosed vehicle for long periods of time. These bows commonly have wood and/or fiberglass laminations, and excessive heat

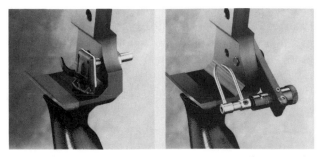

Buy a quality arrow rest; two common styles are shown.

may cause the glue between the component layers to melt, ruining the bow. Some compound bows with solid-metal limbs and risers may also warp just enough to destroy accuracy.

25. The key to shooting accuracy is acquiring an intimate familiarity with your equipment, and this means regular practice throughout the year. Practice your shooting in small, untiring doses; it's far more beneficial to practice for 20 minutes every day of the week than to engage in a single four-hour marathon session on a Saturday morning.

26. How many pins do you need on your bow sight? Some hunters have only one, set at 20 yards. They then restrict themselves to shots of no more than 30 yards, which makes the slight aiming adjustment easy. Other hunters use four pins set at 10-yard intervals. It's a matter of individual preference.

27. Compound-bow hunters often own two identical bows, one of which is kept in camp as a backup. The reason is that it's very difficult to replace a compound bow's broken cable or string in the field; most such bows must be repaired at an archery shop with a bow press. Meanwhile, a backup bow set up exactly the same way as the damaged bow can save an otherwise ended hunt.

28. Wear an arm guard in cold weather when you're bulked up with heavier clothing. Otherwise, a released bowstring may slap against the sleeve of your bow arm and send the arrow flying wildly away.

29. A belt pouch can be used to support the lower limb and wheel assembly of your compound bow. When you're standing, you won't have to constantly strain your muscles by trying to hold your bow vertically, ready to draw and shoot. Moreover, when the moment of truth arrives and a deer is within shooting range, the only movement necessary is raising the bow a few inches to clear the pouch; such minimal movement will reduce the chances of alerting the deer to your presence.

30. Broadheads weighing 100 to 135 grains are recommended for most whitetail deer hunting situations.

31. As a rule, the best fletching twist for right-handed bowhunters is right helical; for left-handed bowhunters, left helical. In either case, 4-inch-long fletching is recommended for stabilizing a car-

bon arrow with a broadhead; 5-inch fletching works best for aluminum arrows fitted with broadheads. Far less satisfactory results come from using straight fletching or fletching that's less than 4 inches long and intended solely for competitive shooting with target points.

32. If your turkey-feather fletching becomes matted or bent due to exposure to moisture, allow it to dry thoroughly. Next, hold it briefly over the steam coming from a teakettle spout, which will allow the feather fronds to spring back to their original shape.

33. Many bowhunters think they can gain greater arrow speed—and thus a flatter arrow trajectory in flight—by increasing a bow's draw weight. This is true, but all bows have an upper draw-weight limit, and in all cases the higher the limit selected, the more difficult the string is to draw and hold. One solution is to use an overdraw, a shelf that extends back from the bow handle. This shelf allows you to use arrows that are shorter and therefore lighter in weight, increasing your arrows' speed and flattening their trajectory without increasing draw weight.

34. When you're using a recurve or long bow, deaden the twanging sound your bowstring makes upon release by tying two acrylic yarn puffs or rubber cat whiskers onto your string, one of them 10 inches from the top limb and the other 10 inches from the bottom. With an overly noisy compound bow, you may have to use four silencers: two on the string and two on the cable.

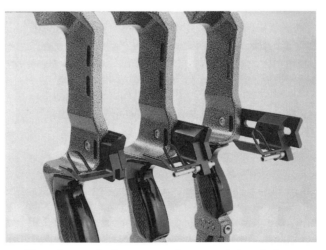

Overdraw shelves come in a variety of sizes.

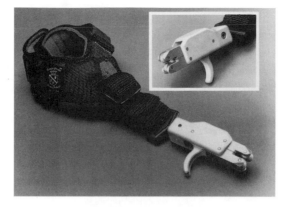

A mechanical bowstring release is generally smoother than shooting with a glove or tab, and it yields greater accuracy. But you must occasionally maintain it by removing grit and grime from the moving parts.

35. If you use a shooting tab or three-fingered glove, small traces of perspiration and grime will eventually roughen the leather's surface, and this will begin to cause a stuttered string release that impairs accuracy. To cure this, place a teaspoon of unscented talcum powder in your hunting jacket pocket, and occasionally place your shooting hand in the pocket. A tab or glove with a fine coating of powder will give you the silkiest shooting release imaginable.

36. If you shoot with a mechanical shooting release, use a can of compressed air to blow out dust, pocket lint, and other debris that's sure to have accumulated in the trigger mechanism. Then add one drop of unscented oil to the inner moving parts.

37. The weakest part of any bow is its string, due to minor but continual fraying. To prolong the string's life, rub it with beeswax several times each season. Put some on your fingertips and then vigorously rub the string between them until you can feel heat being generated, which means the wax is softening and penetrating the strands. Whenever you have any doubt about the string's integrity, immediately replace it; you *do* have a spare on hand, don't you?

38. One advantage that carbon arrows have over aluminum shafts is that they cannot be inadvertently bent; either they remain perfectly straight, or they break. Aluminum shafts become bent from shooting, penetrating a deer, or hitting the ground when a shot is missed. You should either discard damaged arrows or have your local archery shop put the shafts on an aluminum-arrow straightener.

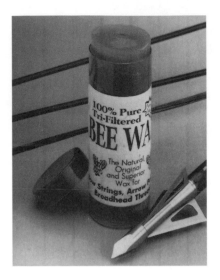

Get into the habit of applying beeswax to your bowstring several times a year.

39. If you plan to build one or more ground blinds, buy a roll of lightweight camouflage cloth. Inexpensive and available in all the popular patterns and colors, the cloth can be cut to length and thumbtacked between two trees. A few strategically placed branches help break up the blind's rectangular shape; all you have to add is a stool to sit on.

40. What's the longest shooting distance a bowhunter should attempt? Only the distance that he has regularly practiced and at which he is confident he can execute with accuracy.

Carbon arrows won't bend; they're either straight, or they break.

14

43 Tips for Rifle Hunters

Accuracy at any range is critical to the rifle hunter. Choosing the right calibers, firearm actions, bullet designs, and scopes all come into play.

1. The ever-unpredictable human element is the most important component in any rifle-shooting equation. Virtually any brand or caliber of rifle taken right from the box, secured in a ballistic lab's vise, and fed with standard factory loads will be more accurate than 99 percent of all the hunters afield. When a live deer is in your sights, and you must estimate the distance instantly and then shoot offhand through cover with poor lighting conditions and pumping adrenaline, pinpoint shooting accuracy can quickly go down the drain. So don't believe the hype that buying a new gun in a different caliber will instantly turn you into an expert marksman. There's a lot more to it than that.

2. Most rifle authorities will tell you that the four calibers best suited to whitetail hunting are the .243 Winchester, .270 Winchester, .30-06 Springfield, and .308 Winchester. Many other calibers can get the job done just as well, but the above four are far and away the most popular—accounting for more than 80 percent of all centerfire rifle sales.

3. When shooting the calibers recommended in tip 2, 100-grain bullets are considered best for the .243; for the .270 I use 130- or 140-grain bullets; and for the .30-06 and .308 I recommend 150- or 165-grain bullets.

The most popular calibers for whitetail hunting are the .243 Winchester, .270 Winchester, .30-06 Springfield, and .308 Winchester.

Firearm experts recommend that whitetail hunters use jacketed bullets in which most of the lead, except for the tip, is covered with a tough alloyed metal.

4. Most proficient hunters rely upon jacketed bullets—also known as controlled expanding bullets—in which most of the lead, except for the tip, is covered with a tough alloyed metal, or where the tip has a thin coat of metal but is notched or has a tiny hollowpoint to facilitate rapid expansion. In either case the jacket gives the bullet good accuracy, performance, and penetration, allowing the bullet to hold together on impact but then quickly begin peeling back from the tip and flattening as it opens a large path. Two examples of such bullets are the Winchester Pointed Soft-Point and the Remington Core-Lokt.

5. When you're hunting, don't use full-jacketed bullets. They invariably pass entirely through a deer, leaving only a small hole and sometimes not inflicting enough collateral shock or tissue damage to prove fatal. Full-jacketed bullets are designed to hold together on impact and penetrate deeply through tough muscle and thick bones before beginning to expand. They're intended for game animals much larger than deer, such as elk, moose, brown bears, and large African species.

6. For a variety of reasons, different regions of the country have become associated with different rifle actions. Throughout the northern border states and into the East and Northeast, for example, the most popular actions seem to be the lever-action

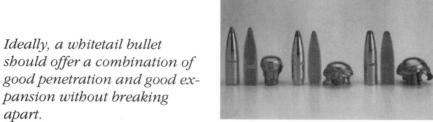

Ideally, a whitetail bullet should offer a combination of good penetration and good expansion without breaking apart.

and the autoloader. In the plains, western, and southwestern states, many hunters carry either a bolt-action or lever-action. And in the Midwest, South, and Southeast, you'll see mostly autoloaders, with someone in the crowd occasionally carrying a pump gun. There are pockets where the rules don't hold, of

Lever-action rifles and open iron sights dominated hunting for decades but are quickly fading from the scene. Lever-action mechanisms are not as strong as the popular bolt-action. And iron sights limit your shooting distance to 100 yards.

The Whitetail Deer Hunter's Almanac

course, but in any case there is no advantage to being a conformist. Regional firearm choices are almost always dictated by tradition, not technical applications.

7. The bolt-action is the most accurate of all the actions, which is why it is unanimously chosen by match shooters and varminters, who typically require precision accuracy at long ranges. It's also the most rugged, the most trouble-free, and the easiest to break down for cleaning, even in the field.

8. If you're in the market for a bolt-action, get one with a 22- or 24-inch barrel. These two lengths account for 95 percent of all bolt-action sales. Some brands may offer slightly longer barrels, but they don't afford noticeably better accuracy at deer hunting's customary shooting distances, and they can be unwieldy in thick cover.

9. A bolt-action rifle intended for whitetail hunting should weigh no more than 7 or 8 pounds. If you add the scope with its base and rings, the rifle suddenly weighs 9 pounds. Then there's the weight of the sling and fully loaded magazine to consider. Remember, additional ounces here and there can feel like pounds when you're climbing steep terrain. If the total weight of your shooting equipment can be kept close to 10 pounds, you've done a good job.

10. The pump gun (slide-action) is not as accurate as the bolt-action, but many hunters find it faster to use. This is because they can quickly chamber additional rounds by simply working the slide in a straight-back/straight-forward manner, as opposed to working a bolt in a 90-degree right-angle eject direction and then working it again in a 90-degree cartridge-feed direction. If you decide on a pump gun, go with the popular 22-inch barrel length. Stripped down, such rifles weigh 7 pounds or so, which means that a fully outfitted firearm will tip the scales at 9 or 10 pounds.

11. The lever-action is especially popular with those who prefer to stillhunt or drive deer, as opposed to stand hunting. Being continually on the move, such hunters need a rifle that still feels light at the end of the day. Barrel lengths average 18 to 20 inches; when stripped down, most lever-actions weigh 5½ to 6½ pounds. The lever-action design allows fast use but, as in the case of the pump gun, it isn't as strong or accurate as the bolt-action.

12. The autoloader (or semi-automatic) isn't impressively accurate. It isn't overly rugged, either; feeding and extraction malfunctions or jams are common when the firearm is not immaculately clean, whenever the weather is unusually cold, and sometimes when you're working with handloads. Barrels average 18 to 22 inches in length. Stripped-down autoloaders weigh in the vicinity of 7½ pounds. The autoloader's deficiencies are compensated for by the fact that its action is by far the fastest; all you need do is repeatedly squeeze the trigger, and the rifle's action will rapidly do the rest.

13. Iron and aperture-type peep sights are waning in popularity, except perhaps among a small contingent of hunters who exclusively stage drives or hunt deer in very thick cover where short shots are the rule. On the plus side, iron sights and aperture-type peep sights are extremely rugged, almost entirely fail-safe, and relatively inexpensive.

14. Because they don't magnify anything, iron sights and aperture-type peep sights generally restrict you to shooting distances of less than 100 yards, which means you'll never be able to take advantage of the long-range capabilities of the four calibers described earlier. The Weaver Scope Company once had a ballistic lab compare a rifle's performance first with a scope and then with open sights; in both tests, exactly the same slugs were used. The scoped rifle offered a 35 percent increase in accuracy at 100 yards, an 85 percent increase at 200 yards, and a whopping 400 percent increase in accuracy at 250 yards!

15. Many hunters err by using scopes of greater magnification than the shooting situation warrants. With any scope, the higher the power, the more restricted the field of view at closer ranges; many times this prevents you from quickly finding your target and centering the reticle on it. This is especially the case when a deer is on the move in cover. Likewise, since the higher magnifications tend to reflect the slightest of normal body tremors (such as excited breathing), holding steady on a faraway target is sometimes futile.

16. For decades standard-field, fixed-power scopes such as the venerable 4X outsold all others. These are still adequate, but today's deer hunters much prefer the various types of wide-angle, variable-magnification scopes.

17. The most popular wide-angle, variable-magnification scope is the 2.5 x 8X. Its versatility is its hallmark. When you're stillhunting, waiting on stand in heavy cover, or participating in drives—all of which are likely to present shots as close as 25 yards—the scope remains on its lowest magnification setting. Yet if you change location to watch a cover edge at a somewhat longer distance—say, 100 yards—a midrange setting can be instantly selected. If you move yet again to watch even more distant terrain (out to 250 yards or so), just bring the highest magnification setting into use.

18. In addition to enlarging the target image, scopes allow you to take greater care in picking your shots in heavy cover. In other words, you're better able to find small openings and tight shooting alleys through tangled branches and vines, which is seldom possible when using open iron sights at distances beyond 50 yards. This reduces the risk that a tiny, unnoticed branch will deflect the rifle bullet, perhaps wounding the animal or missing it altogether.

19. Many optics companies offer light-gathering scopes in their line-ups. This means that a target's resolution, or degree of brightness, is far greater through the scope than what the human eye can ordinarily discern. By utilizing an oversized bell (the scope's front, objective lens), the scope channels a greater quantity of available light back through the ocular lens, or eyepiece. The advantage of this feature is that you can see your target more clearly during the hours of dawn and dusk, in the shade of deep cover, and during inclement weather; this serves as not only a hunting aid but also a safety feature that helps ensure positive target identification.

20. Optics companies offer many types of reticles for deer hunting. Most hunters favor some type of crosshair configuration rather than a post or dot reticle, which can obscure too much of the target at longer ranges. Crosshair reticles are available in fine, medium-fine, and coarse thicknesses. For deer hunting, avoid the fine crosshair variety, which can be difficult to use in thick cover or low-light situations.

21. In the category of crosshair reticles, the most popular are the so-called 4-Plex, Dual-X, or DuPlex designs, in which the thick outer wires of the crosshairs taper down either gradually or abruptly to medium-fine at the center. This design quickly

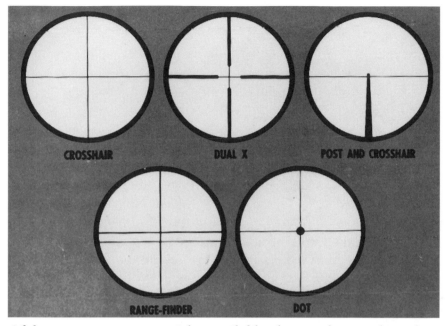

Of the numerous scope reticles available, the crosshair and Dual-X are the best for most shooting applications.

draws the eye to the target and permits easy centering of the crosshairs without obscuring the aiming point.

22. Rangefinder scopes are generally of interest only to those hunters who hunt in regions where shots at deer typically are at long range and across open ground. By using a scale seen through the glass and a calibrated dial on the side of the scope, you can first judge the distance to the deer and then manually adjust the crosshairs so that aiming calculations can be more precise. In this manner, you won't need to guess at how much holdover to use when a deer is in the distance.

23. In mounting a scope, base, and rings, *tight* is the key word. It's also a good practice to check the mounting screws periodically throughout the hunting season. Lab tests have shown that if any of the three telescopic sight components can be wiggled just $\frac{1}{100}$ inch, it will translate into a shot that's off as much as 100 inches at 100 yards.

24. Most companies are doing away with scope-mounting bases and rings that are held in place with slot-type screw heads. As

Scope rings with hex-head screws are far more secure and pleasing to the eye than those with slot-type screws.

you begin to tighten such screws, the screwdriver is prone to slip and either strip the screw-head slot or scratch the finish. In their place, most manufacturers are opting for scope-mounting screws with recessed hex heads that can be tightened only with an Allen wrench. Not only are these more pleasing to the eye, but they can be tightened securely with no damage to the screw, scope, mounting parts, or firearm itself.

25. Scope hardware is often shipped from the factory with a fine coating of lubricant to prevent rust. For the tightest possible scope mounting, it's essential to remove this slippery film. Simply go over all the parts with a toothbrush and small dish of solvent, then dry with a soft rag.

26. When you're mounting the scope base and rings, treat each threaded screw with a droplet of Gun-Tite adhesive, available in any store that sells firearms. This adhesive helps hold the screws in place despite constant recoil and barrel vibrations.

27. Sighting-in a deer rifle is easier if it's first bore-sighted with an optical collimator. Any gunsmith can do this in five minutes at a minimal charge, but if you own a number of firearms, you may wish to buy your own. A bore-sighter fits into the firearm's muzzle; the scope's crosswires are then adjusted to match those in the collimator. This allows you to immediately get bullets on paper rather than having to take many guess shots. Once the collimator has been removed, you can fine-tune your rifle's accuracy.

28. On the range, there's another important step to take before your first fine-tuning shot. Virtually all scopes have a rear, ocular lens that can be adjusted to accommodate any hunter's par-

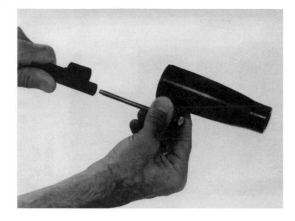

Use an optical collimator to bore-sight the firearm prior to going to the target range to sight-in a deer rifle.

ticular visual deficiencies. Yet some hunters, strangely, never use this eyepiece feature. Do it. It's as easy as focusing binoculars, and will give you a much sharper image of your aim point. Once the eyepiece focusing ring is tightened, it stays that way permanently—until your vision changes or someone borrows your gun and changes the settings.

29. After the ocular lens has been adjusted to your personal vision, check for proper eye relief, which is the distance from the scope eye to the ocular or rear of the scope. A scope that's mounted too far forward in its rings doesn't allow a complete sight picture; loosen the scope rings a bit and slide the scope to the rear until you get a clear and complete sight picture. A scope that's too far to the rear, on the other hand, may clout you in the eyebrow region when the rifle recoils. For most hunters, proper eye relief is somewhere between 2½ and 4 inches.

30. Fine-tuning a rifle's accuracy should *always* be done on a shooting bench with the firearm cradled in sandbags. Never try to sight-in a rifle or any other firearm by holding it offhand; you simply won't get the stability necessary for consistent, accurate shooting. This is due to normal body tremor, breathing fluctuations, and every hunter's inability to hold a firearm perfectly steady without any means of artificial support. The result is erratic shot placement.

31. If you need to check your rifle's accuracy in a camp with no shooting bench or sandbags, the hood of a vehicle is a good alternative. Support the firearm in a cradle of rolled-up blankets

A shooting bench and sandbags are essential for optimum accuracy.

or towels, cut two V-slots in opposite ends of a cardboard box, or rest the rifle on a backpack or even a hunting coat.

32. On the target range, a firearm's accuracy is fine-tuned by turning the windage and elevation knobs on the scope. Each time you make a scope adjustment, fire a three-shot group. Then rest the rifle for at least five minutes to allow the barrel to cool down. As a barrel becomes hotter and hotter (sometimes too hot to touch), accuracy deteriorates noticeably. Besides, when leveling your sights on a deer, your first (and hopefully only) shot will be from a cold barrel, so you want the utmost in cold-barrel accuracy.

33. Most whitetail hunters sight-in their rifles so that, on the target range, the bullets print dead-on (center of bull's-eye) at 25 yards. This should put the slugs approximately 3 inches high of the point of aim at 100 yards, and approximately dead-on again

Shot at the upper left-hand square, this first group is low and to the right. Ideally it should be 3 inches above the square and moved left by one inch.

at 200 yards. Of course, bullet weight and the caliber of the firearm may skew these figures slightly. Why this particular sighting-in formula? Because a deer's 12-inch by 12-inch lung region is the ideal aiming point. With this formula, you can hold dead-on at any range from point blank to 250 yards and still be sure you'll connect with the chest cavity.

34. To make the rifle shoot higher or lower, the scope's elevation knob is adjusted; adjustments to the right or left are made by turning the windage knob. Most such knobs have arrows on them, indicating the direction to turn the dials if you want the point of impact to be raised, lowered, or sent to the right or left. Both knobs are also graduated in click stops, with each click representing an angle of .25 minute (at 100 yards, 1 minute of angle is 1 inch).

35. If slugs are consistently printing 1 inch high at 100 yards (which is 2 inches below the desired point of impact), turn your elevation knob up by eight clicks.

36. If slugs are consistently printing 4 inches to the left of point of aim, turn your windage knob 16 clicks to the right.

37. What's considered good accuracy for a conventional (noncustomized) deer rifle? As a rule, at 100 yards 2-inch groups are considered acceptable, 1½-inch groups are very good, and 1-inch groups bestow bragging rights upon the shooter.

38. Get into the habit of regularly cleaning your scope's lenses. Otherwise, a gradual buildup of dust and grime will reduce the sharpness of the image you see through the optics. Avoid using the common spit-and-handkerchief method, because dust or grit embedded in the cloth's fibers may scratch the lenses. Instead, use the same lens-cleaning fluid and tissue that photographers use on their expensive camera lenses.

39. When hunting in inclement weather, many hunters use scope covers. These are rubber or plastic affairs that quickly fit over the front and rear ends of the scope to keep the lenses free from rain and snow, and to prevent the glass from fogging. They can be quickly removed when you want to take a shot.

40. Every deer rifle should be outfitted with a sling, which lets you shoulder the firearm while you navigate steep or slippery terrain. Those with extra-wide straps are the most popular, be-

Use lens covers that flip up instantly if you're expecting rain or snow.

cause they stay on your shoulder and don't cut into your skin when you're hunting in warm weather and wearing light clothing.

41. Most rifle triggers come from the factory preset at anywhere from 4 to 6 pounds, which is difficult enough to squeeze (for safety reasons) that accuracy can be affected. A much smoother and crisper trigger pull is around 2 or 3 pounds. The creep, or distance the trigger must travel before the sear is released to discharge the round, should likewise be removed. If you can't do this work yourself, have your gunsmith make the adjustments.

42. Never climb up or down from a tree stand with a rifle slung over your shoulder and a cartridge in the chamber. Always use a haul rope to raise and lower the firearm, and always tie the rope to the *rear* sling swivel, so the rifle's muzzle is pointing downward.

43. When you're preparing to take a shot, use a rest whenever possible to stabilize the firearm and increase accuracy. If you're shooting from a prone position, you can do this by cradling the firearm in the crook of a western hat or in a piece of clothing.

Bipods, such as this Harris model, are excellent for hunting while prone, sitting, or kneeling. The legs extend out to 3 feet in length; when the legs are collapsed, they fold up against the forearm for easy carrying.

You can also attach a bipod to the rifle's forearm. In a sitting position, lay the rifle's forearm on your upturned palm placed on a raised knee. If you're kneeling, use two cross sticks (several companies make excellent ones). If you're standing, lean against a tree trunk. However, when you take any kind of rest, make sure that the rifle's forearm is always resting on something that provides a cushioning effect. Never lay the forearm on a rigid, hard surface such as a boulder, which will cause shots to fly higher than your point of aim. This occurs because the hard surface exerts slight upward pressure on the stock forearm, which in turn exerts slight upward pressure on the free-floating barrel.

15

36 Tips for
Slug-Shotgun Hunters

*How to get the most from the new high-tech
shotguns.*

1. The past 10 years have seen tremendous strides in deer-shotgun technology. It's a good thing, too, because some state wildlife agencies are predicting that only shotguns will be legal for deer hunting east of the Mississippi by the year 2020. With more and more people moving to the country, short-range shotguns are simply safer than long-range centerfire rifles in many situations. When fired at a 30-degree angle of elevation, some centerfire rifle bullets may travel as much as several miles, while the maximum range of most 12-gauge shotgun slugs is only about 2,400 feet.

2. Just because slug shotguns are short-range firearms, don't mistakenly assume that their accuracy leaves anything to be desired. Ballistic tests have shown that a finely tuned modern shotgun equipped with a scope is more accurate than many venerable deer rifles of a generation ago, including the .30–30 Winchester, .35 Remington, .32 Winchester Special, and .44 Magnum.

3. The only reasonable bore to use for deer shotgunning is the 12-gauge. All others fall far behind in terms of deer-slug performance. A 1-ounce Foster-type slug leaves the barrel of a 12-

Short-range slug shotguns are increasingly being required for deer in populous areas—and states.

gauge with a velocity of only 1,600 feet per second but possesses a walloping 2,485 foot-pounds of energy. Thus it packs the same amount of knockdown power as a 150-grain, .30–06 bullet at 50 yards. Other slugs, such as the 12-gauge 3-inch magnum Brenneke Golden at a hefty 600 grains, have a muzzle energy of 2,913 foot-pounds of energy, giving them the same smack as a 150-grain, .30–06 bullet at 100 yards!

4. Ballistics tests have revealed that in most 12-gauge deer shotguns, 3-inch-magnum loads are less accurate than standard 2¾-inch loads. And the additional recoil is torture. Until the Federal Bureau of Ballistic Standards raises the allowable chamber pressure in shotguns beyond the current 12,500 feet per square inch—to accommodate the extra extenders in the longer shells and the greater amount of powder being burned—stick with standard 2¾-inch loads.

5. For hunters, the least-desirable deer-shotgun action is the break-open single-shot. This doesn't mean that those currently on the market are of poor quality. It's simply that the procedure of cocking the hammer takes practice if you're to avoid making an audible click that may spook deer. Also, since there's little or no receiver length on which to mount a scope, you must be satisfied with open rifle-type sights. Plus, of course, you've got only one shot. However, most brands on the market are nevertheless fine starter guns for youngsters or first-time older hunters. This is because their single-shot capability and uncomplicated loading and unloading make them very safe and easy to master for those who don't have much firearm experience.

6. Deer hunters should also avoid double-barrel shotguns such as over-and-unders and side-by-sides. Because of the canted way in which the barrels are married to the receiver, slugs fired from doubles cross over during their trajectories. In other words, with a side-by-side, a slug fired from the left barrel will, on a target, print to the right of a slug fired from the right barrel, and vice versa. Similarly, with an over-and-under, a slug from the bottom barrel will print higher than a slug from the top barrel, and vice versa. You can add to this confusion the fact that the two barrels of over-and-unders and side-by-sides are nearly always of different chokes, which also results in erratic slug flight. Finally, scopes and aperture-type peep sights cannot be mounted on these firearms, and any semblance of accuracy us-

ing only a front bead sight is reduced to pure guesswork. For deer hunting, avoid these shotguns entirely.

7. Bolt-action shotguns, such as the famous Tar-Hunt and Browning A-Bolt, are currently the state of the art in whitetail slug hunting. They're every bit as high in quality as branded centerfire rifles. The downside is that they usually carry price tags as much as three times higher than autoloading and pump shotguns.

8. Autoloading and pump shotguns offer a five-round capacity but, increasingly, states are passing laws requiring the use of a plug in the magazine tube that reduces the capacity to three rounds. If you don't have a plug or one didn't come with your new firearm, it's not necessary to order one from the manufacturer. Simply cut a piece of ¾-inch-diameter dowel rod to 5 inches long and insert it into the tube.

9. One disadvantage of autoloading shotguns is that feeding and ejection problems can occur, especially in cold or inclement weather. Also, if you wish to mount a scope on an autoloader, expect to run into difficulties. Most autoloader receivers are made of aluminum. When the thin metal on the top of the receiver is drilled and tapped, screws cannot be embedded deeply enough or subsequently tightened enough to securely hold a scope mount.

10. Some shooters try to solve the shotgun scope-mounting dilemma by buying a slug barrel that has a scope dovetail mount welded right where it fits into the receiver. But this usually works out poorly, because the scope ends up being mounted so far forward that its eye relief is substantially increased, which prevents you from gaining a full sight picture. It's better to purchase the type of aftermarket slug barrel that has a cantilever scope mount. The cantilever is welded to the rear of the barrel just like a dovetail scope mount, but it incorporates a shelflike device that extends still farther to the rear. The scope is mounted onto this shelf, allowing for an acceptable eye-relief distance. Another option is to buy a scope mount that attaches to the side of the receiver; the gunsmith will still have to drill into soft aluminum, but it's thicker on the side of the receiver than on top.

11. Pump shotguns are far and away the most popular with whitetail hunters. They're ruggedly built and virtually fail-safe in oper-

The receivers of many shotguns are made of thin aluminum that cannot be drilled and tapped for secure scope mounting. One alternative is an aftermarket slug barrel with a cantilever scope shelf that extends back over the receiver.

ation. Moreover, their receivers are usually made of case-hardened steel, allowing you to drill and tap a strong scope mount.

12. With smoothbore shotguns, a deer slug will pass through all types of muzzle choke constrictions without damage to the firearm. But you sacrifice a great deal of accuracy if you use an

The most popular slug gun is the 12-gauge pump. This is Ithaca's Deerslayer with a Hastings aftermarket rifled barrel and a 2 x 8X Bausch & Lomb scope.

improved-cylinder, modified, or full choke. It's better to use a cylinder choke (which has the least constriction); better still, if available, is an optional, interchangeable slug barrel with a straight bore (no choke at all).

13. When you obtain an interchangeable slug barrel to replace your shot-pellet barrel, it will come equipped with rifle-type sights. These usually consist of a front elevated blade on a ramp and some kind of adjustable, notched rear sight. But most hunters who invest in a slug barrel want maximum performance, and this means mounting a scope on the receiver.

14. When you're using a smoothbore shotgun, use only Foster-style slugs, which have a weighty nose section and a hollow base and fly much the same as a badminton shuttlecock. Contrary to what some hunters believe, the helical fins on Foster-style slugs do not impart any degree of spin that might increase accuracy; they simply allow the slug to squeeze through any size of choke constriction in the shotgun barrel. It's the weighty nose section that stabilizes the slug in flight and keeps it in line with the aiming point.

15. The most popular Foster-type slugs are made by Winchester, Federal, and Remington, and range in weight from 435 to 547 grains. Buckshot loads are not recommended, because of their

Left to right: the Winchester Foster-style, BRI-500, Remington Foster-style, and Brenneke shotgun slugs.

Use only sabot slugs for optimum performance in deer shotguns fitted with rifled barrels.

garden-hose spraying effect; four states allow the use of buckshot.

16. A variation on the Foster-style slug has a fiber wad attached to its base, in the belief that this will enhance stability in flight. The jury is still out on this speculation. The most common examples are made by Brenneke and Activ, and range in weight from 492 to 600 grains.

17. When you're using a high-tech deer shotgun with a factory-installed rifled barrel, or when you're removing a smoothbore barrel from a shotgun and slipping on an aftermarket rifled barrel for deer hunting, always use a sabot (pronounced SAY-boh) slug. This is a slug encased in a two-part plastic sleeve. When fired, internal gas pressure causes the plastic-sleeve assembly to expand and grip the barrel's inner lands and grooves. This phenomenon causes the slug to exit the muzzle with near-perfect gyroscopic stability. It also imparts spin to the slug, and—as with a centerfire rifle bullet—a spinning shotgun slug is far more accurate than one that doesn't spin. After traveling about 20 yards from the muzzle, the lightweight, two-part sabot meets air resistance and falls away while the slug continues on.

18. The most popular sabot slugs are made by Winchester, Federal, Remington, and Lightfield, and range in weight from 423 to 485 grains.

19. Since various sabot slugs come in different weights, it's best to experiment with several brands to determine which fares best in a particular shotgun. If you eventually decide to switch to a different brand of slug with a different weight than your current brand, you should sight-in your gun to see if any slight adjustments are necessary. The same holds true when you're switching between any of the Foster-type or Foster-Attached-Wad slugs.

20. There's a consensus among deer shotgunners that the ideal weight for a high-tech slug gun (be it a bolt-action, autoloader, or pump) is between 7 and 8 pounds. Add a scope mount, scope, and sling, then fill the magazine with slugs, and the firearm approaches 10 pounds . . . the same weight as the ideal deer rifle. When you're considering different brands of guns, keep in mind the recommended barrel length of 20 to 24 inches.

21. Which brand, style, and weight of shotgun slug is best for deer? Since virtually all of them are of high quality, this is a tough decision. It sounds unscientific, but each shotgun has its own personality and will therefore shoot certain types of slugs better than others. I watched one hunter sighting-in with Remington-Foster slugs, and at 100 yards the best he could achieve was 5-inch groups. When he switched to nearly identical Winchester-Foster slugs, though, his groups tightened up to nearly half that. Another hunter's experience was that neither Remington-Foster nor Winchester-Foster slugs yielded acceptable performance in his slug gun, but he was amazed with the accuracy of Federal-Foster slugs and Brennekes. Buy a small quantity of all brands, head for the range, and allow your shotgun to decide what it likes.

22. What's the best downrange performance you can expect from a smoothbarrel deer shotgun with Foster-style slugs and aperture-type or peep sights? Generally, you'll be doing well if you shoot 4-inch groups at 75 yards, and your shooting distance should be restricted to 100 yards.

23. What's the best downrange performance you can expect from a smoothbarrel deer shotgun with Foster-type slugs and a scope?

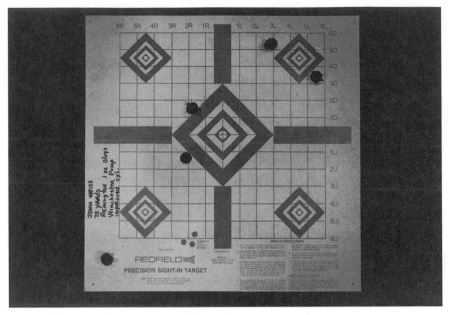

Every shotgun has a personality all its own, so it pays to range-test several different types of slugs to determine which performs best in your firearm. This group was not acceptable.

Generally, you'll do well to shoot 3-inch groups at 100 yards; restrict your shooting distance to no more than 125 yards.

24. What's the best downrange performance you can expect from a rifled barrel shotgun with sabot slugs and a scope? Generally, you'll do well to shoot 1½-inch groups at 100 yards, with the shooting distance restricted to 150 yards.

25. The information about scopes and scope-mounting procedures in chapter 14, 43 Tips for Rifle Hunters, applies almost entirely to slug shotguns as well. There is one exception. A wide-angle scope with variable magnification is still suggested for slug shotguns, but the magnification need not be as high, simply because the maximum recommended shooting distance is only 150 yards. This means a scope of 1.5 x 3X or 2.5 x 5X is fine. Also, in accordance with rifle-scope recommendations, a Dual-X crosshair reticle is favored by most hunters. This is the type in which the thick outer extremities of the crosshairs taper either gradually or abruptly to medium-fine at the center.

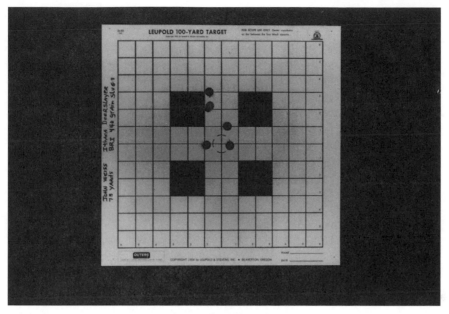

This first group at 75 yards, with sabot slugs, is acceptable, but testing other slugs and a bit of fine-tuning could improve it.

26. Sighting-in a slug shotgun using rifle-type sights or an aperture-type peep sight is most commonly done by adjusting the rear sight up or down and sideways. The rule of thumb is to always move the rear sight in the direction you want the slug to go. In other words, if slugs are printing to the left of the bull's-eye, move the rear sight to the left. If slugs are printing lower than you'd like, lower the rear sight. However, since there are so many open-sight variations on the market, consult the manufacturer's instructions for more specific information.

27. In addition to adjustable rear sights, some aftermarket barrels also have adjustable front blade sights mounted in dovetails. This allows them to be moved right or left by lightly tapping on them with a hammer and small centerpunch tool.

28. Sighting-in a deer shotgun with a scope differs from sighting-in a scoped centerfire rifle in two significant ways. First, the distance capability of even a high-tech shotgun is far less than that of a centerfire rifle, so no allowance need be made for shooting

possibilities beyond 200 yards. Also, rifle bullets fly on a different trajectory than do shotgun slugs. Slugs have a relatively flat trajectory out to about 100 yards, then drop rapidly. Consequently, most deer shotgunners sight-in their scopes so slugs are dead-on (center of bull's-eye) at 25 yards. This also puts them nearly dead-on at the 100-yard target. If you're using a high-tech shotgun with a rifled barrel and sabot slugs, however, you'll have to fire several groups at the maximum recommended 150 yards to determine how much drop occurs in that additional 50 yards; then you need only make a mental note of the amount of drop so you can adjust your holdover if a 150-yard shot presents itself.

29. Slug-shotgun accuracy can be improved significantly by stiffening and lightening the trigger pull. Most shotgun trigger assemblies come from the factory set at 5 or 6 pounds. These heavy-set triggers are designed to be "slapped," not squeezed as with a rifle trigger, so have your gunsmith adjust your slug-gun trigger to a 3-pound pull with little or no travel.

30. If your particular slug gun's trigger cannot be adjusted to a lower-pound pull and its creep cannot be removed, consider buying an aftermarket, fully adjustable, rifle-type trigger assembly. It can be installed in minutes.

31. The weakest part of any shotgun is the linkup where the barrel is attached to the receiver. In some cases, the barrel screws into the receiver; in other cases, it twists in and locks with several lugs. In either case, it's often a sloppy, imprecise fit. This matters little when you're shooting at a pheasant or rabbit, but it can cause problems when you're trying to achieve deer-slug accuracy. Ask your gunsmith if he can remedy this problem with your specific firearm by using epoxy or some other method; if he can, be forewarned that the change will probably be permanent. You'll now have a full-time deer shotgun . . . but one that is far more accurate than before.

32. It's especially important to thoroughly clean a slug shotgun at the end of the season. Foster-type slugs are made of very soft lead that will foul a smooth barrel as quickly as lead shot will. Saboted slugs are equally damaging, but in their case it's the plastic sabot sleeves that leave residue on the lands and grooves of rifled barrels. In either case, use a quality barrel solvent and stiff-bristle brass cleaning brush to do the job.

This buck was shot as it tried to sneak through a funnel leading to heavy cover.

33. In regions where slug shotguns are mandated, you can be sure there's a relatively large human population. This means more hunting pressure, so it's probably futile to set up a stand or blind overlooking a feeding area such as a field, hay meadow, or low-growing cropland. Pressured deer simply won't venture into such open places, except after dark. Your best bet is to scout the heaviest cover you can find, especially funnels and travel corridors that deer will use to evade hunters.

34. Since pressured deer circle and dodge hunters all day, dusk and dawn aren't the only productive times to see animals. Shotgun deer hunters accept the fact that they're just as likely to see a buck sneaking through their area at noon as at morning's first light. It consequently pays to remain on stand all day.

35. Slug-shotgun hunting is in most states scheduled for later in the year, with the early deer seasons given over to bow- and black-powder hunters. When you scout for food sources, then, keep in mind that foods that are abundant in the early fall may be depleted by the time early winter arrives. Zero in on mast-bearing trees such as oaks and beeches; if the mast crop was normal, there should still be plenty of acorns and beechnuts on the ground when the slug-shotgun season opens. Many farmers will also still have standing corn in their fields late in the year, and this is a magnet to deer. So are abandoned orchards. These food sources should be next to the heavy cover, however, or deer will avoid them during the day.

36. As a rule, tree stands used by slug shotgunners should be placed somewhat higher than stands used earlier in the season with other forms of shooting equipment. The reason is that the leaf drop is complete before most states' slug-shotgunning seasons begin, leaving hunters who are aloft far more exposed. Low stands are acceptable if you can find trees with many gnarled, spreading branches to break up your outline, or if you can place yours in a conifer (which retains its leaves year-round).

50 Blackpowder Hunting Tips

Here's a quick review of things to remember that will ensure trouble-free muzzleloading.

1. When you take your flintlock or percussion-cap rifle out of offseason storage, run several dry patches down the barrel to remove the oily coating that you put there to prevent rust. Otherwise, the oil may deactivate the first powder charge you load and prevent ignition. Use a pipe cleaner to remove oil from the nipple.

2. Place a short strip of tape over the bore to prevent rain or snow from entering the barrel and causing rust or possibly deactivating the powder charge. You can shoot right through the tape with no loss of velocity or accuracy.

3. At the end of a hunting day afield, it's not necessary to discharge your muzzleloader. All states consider the firearm legally unloaded if you simply remove the cap from a percussion rifle or the powder charge from a flintlock's pan.

4. If you use Pyrodex pellets, don't touch them with your fingers; oil or moisture on your skin may lessen the potency of the charge. Included with each box of pellets is a short pipe cleaner designed to slide through each pellet's centerhole for hands-free loading.

5. Always load Pyrodex pellets into the barrel with their blackened ends facing down. This blackening is an accelerant smearing of black powder that, when seated against the percussion cap, ensures full ignition of the Pyrodex.

6. Before you load a percussion-cap rifle, place a clean patch on a ramrod, push it down the barrel, and fire three caps. Then extract the ramrod and patch. You should see a black star pattern on the patch and a burned hole in the center, indicating that any residual oil or cleaning solvent has been blown out of the nipple, nipple port, and breech and that they're clean and dry.

7. As you consider your first purchase of a blackpowder gun for deer hunting, remember that a rifle in .50 caliber is generally considered best for the most situations.

8. For deer hunting, two Pyrodex pellets (equivalent to 100 grains of black powder) are recommended.

9. If you're using black powder, experiment on the target range with loads ranging from 100 to 125 grains to determine which specific charge yields the best accuracy with your chosen bullet.

For whitetail hunting, experts agree that a rifle in .50 caliber is best.

10. Among deer hunters, the most popular .50-caliber bullets for use in the new high-tech in-line and Outer-Line rifles are 250- or 300-grain copper solid hollowpoints or copper solid bullets with lead noses.

11. Every blackpowder hunter carries a possibles bag full of assorted supplies and tools. However, one item that should never

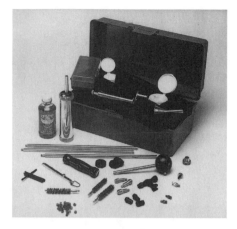

Most hunters carry spare accessories in a small tacklebox in their truck or camp.

go into this bag is your nipple capper. Keep it close at hand on a neck lanyard so you can instantly recap your rifle if a dud cap fails to ignite.

12. When you're hunting, it's not necessary to clean a blackpowder rifle barrel after every shot unless time and convenience allow

To ensure maximum accuracy, clean a muzzleloader's barrel after every shot when you sight-in on the target range.

for it. *Do* clean the barrel after every shot when you're sighting-in on the rifle range, however, to ensure optimum shot-to-shot accuracy.

13. Immediately after you pour a charge of black powder down the barrel of a percussion-cap gun or flintlock, always firmly slap the barrel several times with the palm of your hand. This ensures that all the powder has settled into the breech before you load the bullet.

14. If either a percussion cap or the powder in a flintlock's frizzen ignites but the powder charge in the barrel fails to burn, consider it a misfire and act as though the rifle can fire at any second. Keep the rifle pointed in a safe direction for at least one full minute before you recap the nipple or recharge the pan and attempt to fire again.

15. When you're sighting-in a flintlock or sidelock percussion rifle on the rifle range, make sure there are no bystanders to your immediate right. Flames, sparks, and bits of percussion cap metal or flint chips may spray in that direction.

16. Speed-loaders, each containing a premeasured powder charge and bullet, allow for quick reloading afield. Three or four of them in your possibles bag should be enough for a day of hunting.

17. Heed the old adage about "keeping your powder dry" by loading your rifle at home or in camp, not outside in inclement weather. A rifle preloaded in this manner is safe to handle and legal to transport in a vehicle so long as there is no percussion cap on the nipple or powder in the pan.

18. If you suspect that your powder charge has become deactivated due to moisture or oil in the barrel, unscrew the nipple and trickle a few grains of powder into the nipple port. Then replace the nipple, install a fresh cap, and fire the rifle in a safe direction. The added flash from the additional grains of dry powder is often enough to cause ignition. If not, your only alternative is to unscrew the breech plug and use a ramrod to force the powder and bullet down the length of the barrel and out the bore.

19. When you're ramming a bullet or ball down the barrel, it's critical to seat it firmly against the powder charge. If it's not seated, it's a barrel obstruction and can result in an exploding barrel.

20. The priming powder you use for a flintlock's pan should be exceedingly fine four-F powder, not the coarser double-F variety poured down the barrel.

21. When you're readying a flintlock to fire, pour enough powder into the pan so that it comes up to a level meeting the touch hole but not covering it. The powder is so light that some of it can fall out of the pan even when the frizzen is closed. When you're hunting, then, get into the habit of frequently checking it and adding more powder as necessary.

22. In the most inclement weather, protection should be given the blackpowder rifle's locking area. For a percussion-cap rifle, place a 3-inch square of plastic wrap around the drum and capped nipple, and hold it in place with a twist-tie; you need only cock the hammer and fire without having to remove the plastic.

23. To protect a flintlock in bad weather, buy a molded-plastic hood that covers the entire hammer-pan-frizzen assembly; this protector must be removed before shooting.

24. The most weatherproof, surefire blackpowder ignition system currently on the market is the Markesbery 400 SRP found on Markesbery Outer-Line rifles. The standard nipple is replaced with a two-piece stainless-steel housing. A small rifle primer is placed in the bottom half of the housing; the top half, containing a free-floating firing pin, is then screwed on. The procedure takes only a few seconds, the ignition system is 100 percent waterproof, and the small rifle primer puts 10 times as much fire into the breech as even the hottest percussion cap.

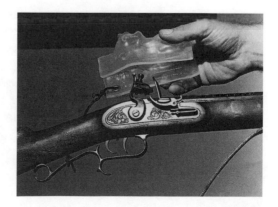

A molded-plastic hood will protect the hammer-pan-frizzen area from rain and snow.

The SRP, from Markesbery Muzzleloaders.

25. Although patched-ball loads will kill deer at ranges out to 75 yards, most hunters like to take advantage of the their muzzleloader's fullest capabilities by using maxi-balls, full-bore conical bullets, jacketed handgun bullets, or saboted bullets. In addition to extending your shooting distance by 50 yards or more, they're easier and faster to load.

26. Each time you discharge a percussion-cap gun, check the hammer's recessed head for deformed remnants of the cap. If left in place, they can dull the hammer's impact on a fresh cap as you take a second shot.

27. In bitter-cold weather, don't bring your blackpowder rifle inside a warm dwelling; condensation may form on interior and exterior metal parts. Simply remove the percussion cap or powder in the pan and stow the rifle in your car trunk, your truck gun rack, or a shed or outbuilding protected from rain and snow.

28. In states where it's legal, most owners of high-tech in-line and Outer-Line muzzleloaders prefer to outfit them with scopes. Since blackpowder rifles are relatively short-range firearms, the most popular scope is a wide-angle model with a variable magnification of 2 x 7X.

29. Few blackpowder hunters completely strip down their rifles and use hot soapy water to clean them. A superior and much

Wide-angle scopes are most popular.

faster cleaning job can be achieved by removing the nipple and breech plug and allowing them to soak in a solvent bath such as Black Off. Meanwhile, run solvent-soaked patches through the bore. When everything is sparkling clean, usually within only 10 minutes, reassemble the components, apply a light coat of protective lubricant, and you're finished!

30. An often overlooked tool that should be in every possibles bag is a patch puller or worm. This is a hooklike snare that screws into the end of the ramrod to retrieve a cleaning patch that has separated from the cleaning jag.

31. Another indispensable accessory is a nipple pick, used to clean fired-cap residue from the nipple hole before a second, fresh cap is installed. A simple safety pin attached to your jacket works just as well for this.

32. If you want to add a scope to your blackpowder rifle, use a quick-detach scope mount and rings. Blackpowder rifles require cleaning far more frequently than centerfire rifles, and a quick-detach mount is not only faster to remove and reinstall but also allows the scope to retain its zero without your having to sight-in the firearm after each cleaning.

33. If you're in the market for a new blackpowder rifle and plan to shoot saboted all-copper bullets or jacketed handgun rounds, pick a model that offers a fast rate of barrel-rifling twist for the best performance; for these bullets, a barrel with a twist of one

Tony Knight, inventor of the famous MK-85 and other Knight rifles, displays one of his newer blackpowder models.

A perfect broadside shot. If you hit him, remember exactly where he was standing, so you can trail him if he runs off.

turn in 26 inches or one in 34 inches is recommended. If you plan to shoot patched round balls or bore-sized conical bullets such as maxi-balls or Buffalo Bullets, a barrel with a twist of one turn in 48 inches or one in 66 inches performs best.

34. Patched balls and all-lead conical bullets that pass entirely through a deer create small entrance and exit holes. As a result, there may be no immediate blood trail. If you hit a deer but can't find the animal or its blood trail, begin walking in increasingly wider back-and-forth arcs from the location where you last saw it. Do this carefully, and chances are you'll discover either the blood or dead animal itself.

35. When you're shopping for a new blackpowder rifle, keep in mind that a 24-inch barrel yields the best overall performance with the widest range of bullet types and powder charges. This is because ballistic tests have shown that a barrel shorter than 24 inches does not allow all of the powder to be burned before the projectile leaves the muzzle. A barrel longer than 24 inches, on the other hand, reduces a projectile's muzzle velocity and foot-pounds of energy.

36. Never pour a powder charge from a can, flask, or powder horn down a barrel. If a smoldering ember is present from your last shot, it could ignite not only the new charge being poured but also the powder in the larger container. It's better, and safer, to

use a small measuring device that holds only the amount of powder to be loaded.

37. Black powder is extremely corrosive, so make sure you clean your firearm thoroughly after each use. A blackpowder rifle put into storage at the end of the hunting season without being cleaned will have a rusted and pitted barrel by the time next year's hunting season opens.

38. If you use a flintlock, check the metal surface of the frizzen frequently. If it begins to develop a bit of scale rust, there will be a reduction in the amount of sparking that occurs when the hammer strikes the flint across the frizzen. A light touch-up with a piece of steel wool (kept in your possibles bag) quickly remedies the problem.

39. When you load a round ball, always center a well-lubed patch on the bore and then position the ball with the sprue "up." (The sprue is the small flat place on the ball created when molten lead is poured during the manufacturing process.)

40. Blackpowder rifles with iron sights are easy to sight-in. The front blade is fixed, so you only have to adjust the rear dovetail up or down, right or left. Fire a three-shot group at a 25-yard target. If the group is right of the bull's-eye, move the rear sight to the right; if you're shooting left, move the rear sight to the left. If the group is low, elevate the rear sight; if it's high, lower the rear sight. Then fine-tune your group at 100 yards.

41. When you're using a ramrod, never grab it more than 8 inches above the muzzle. Doing so will cause severe side stress on the rod, possibly causing it to break and injure your hand.

42. To determine proper load depth, insert the ramrod when the rifle is fully loaded and then use an indelible-ink pen to mark the ramrod at the point where it protrudes from the barrel. This mark now serves as a reference point each time you load. If the mark is above the muzzle, you know the projectile has not been seated deeply enough, causing a dangerous barrel ob-

Markesbery Brown Bear Outer-Line rifle, with iron sights.

struction if fired! Ram the load deeper until it's tight against the powder and the ramrod mark is flush with the bore.

43. When you remove the rifle's percussion cap or the powder from a flintlock's pan at the end of the day, a wise safety measure is to tie a tag on the trigger guard. This informs anyone around that even though the rifle is legally "unloaded," there's still powder and a bullet in the barrel.

44. If you want to cast your own round balls or maxi-balls, use only pure lead. Lead alloys, as used in the manufacture of wheel weights or Linotype from a print shop, contain large amounts of antimony; using this results in very hard projectiles that are difficult to properly load and seat against a powder charge.

45. Pyrodex is *not* recommended for use in flintlock rifles, because it isn't as flammable as black powder. This can substantially increase hang time (a dangerous situation) if frizzen sparks occasionally are not hot or intense enough.

46. Hammer blow back occurs when the hammer is driven back to the half-cock position an instant after the rifle is fired. It's a dangerous occurrence, the result of very high pressure caused by excessive barrel fouling or the use of too much powder. Clean the barrel immediately. Then, before you attempt to fire the rifle again, consult your owner's manual to make sure you're loading the recommended powder charge.

47. When you're sighting-in a rifle with a patched ball, recover a few of the fired patches to learn if they're doing their job; they'll be on the ground about 10 yards in front of the muzzle. A lubed patch that's performing well will be blackened in the center, where it was exposed to the burning powder. A patch that is not only blackened but also burned through either is made of thin, inferior material or wasn't lubed thoroughly.

48. If it's ever necessary to pull a round from a muzzleloader, always deactivate the powder first. The easiest way is to remove the priming powder from a flintlock pan or the nipple from a percussion-cap rifle. Then squirt cleaning solvent into the breech plug, or remove the barrel from the stock and soak the breech area in a bucket of hot water for half an hour.

49. When loading a patched ball, some hunters try to economize by simply spitting on the patch rather than using lube. The trouble

is that a spit patch can dry out in hot weather or freeze in cold weather; both conditions result in poor shooting performance. Lube is cheap. Use it.

50. Many replica blackpowder rifles, such as the Thompson-Center Hawken, have double-set triggers. If you first pull the rear trigger, you "set" the front trigger so that only slight finger pressure is needed to fire the round. To eliminate this two-step firing method, some hunters simply yank the front trigger, but this can destroy the sight picture and cause a miss. Use the set trigger as it was intended.

17

39 Truths About
Deer-Camp Comfort

How to eat well, sleep warm, and have few hassles.

1. If you have a long drive to a deer camp in another state, don't attempt a marathon, nonstop haul. You'll arrive feeling like a zombie. The cumulative effect of each additional day of hunting is tiring enough; don't make it worse by starting off tired on the first day of the hunt. Stop overnight at a motel along the way. Take every opportunity to rest and conserve your energy level. If you do, your spirits will remain higher and you'll be a more effective and successful hunter.

2. If you're traveling with one or more hunting partners in the same vehicle, switch drivers every hour or so, and make a pit stop every two hours. All of you will arrive in camp happy and energetic.

3. When you select a site for your tents, avoid low ground, which usually is moist and may pose insect problems in mild or warm weather. Also avoid high ground such as ridgelines, where the wind is sure to batter your tents. Relatively flat, midelevation terrain is usually best. Before making your final decision, check surrounding trees to make sure none have large, dead limbs that may fall into your living area.

4. If you're in your sleeping bag and feeling cold because your tent or cabin is unheated, you can increase your body warmth by covering your head. A soft wool watch cap is perfect.

5. If you wake up cold in the middle of the night, don't reach for another blanket to cover yourself. Your problem is that your weight is compressing the insulation underneath your body,

A tent camp on flat ground—just the way it should be.

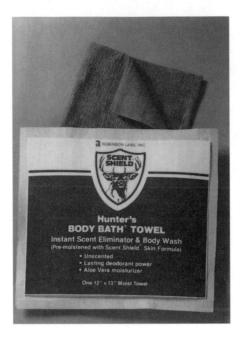

Moistened towelettes are perfect for deer camp.

thus allowing body heat to escape. So fold that extra blanket lengthwise and place it on the cot or ground *beneath* your sleeping bag.

6. Newspaper has amazing insulating properties. If there are no spare blankets in camp, place a thick layer of newspaper under your sleeping bag.

7. Is water scarce in camp and reserved strictly for drinking and cooking? If so, moistened towelettes are ideal for personal hygiene. Put a dozen or so in your duffel bag before leaving home.

8. To dry wet socks and gloves, drape them over the top of a lamp shade and then turn on the bulb. Keep an eye on them so they don't scorch.

9. Do you despise climbing out of your sleeping bag on a bitter-cold morning and having to climb into the cold clothing that's laid out next to your bunk? Place your clothes in the bottom of your sleeping bag when you go to sleep at night and your body heat will keep them toasty. You can also place them on your cot, under your sleeping bag.

10. Trying to light a gasoline or propane lantern in predawn darkness, or at night, can be dangerous. Many hunters who also fish

take their 12-volt trolling-motor battery to camp. Beforehand, they've jury-rigged several small 12-volt lights with wires that lead to the battery's terminals; just one light, of the size used on a motorbike, will illuminate the interior of a four-man tent. A simple in-line toggle switch can be flipped to instantly turn the lights on and off. One light can be attached to the inside peak of the tent with a safety pin, another at the entranceway, and others elsewhere as desired. A charged battery should last all week.

11. If your deer-camp latrine is an open-air affair involving a pit dug in the ground, dig the pit extra deep and leave a small entrenching tool nearby. You can then throw a shovelful of dirt into the pit after each use. When the hunting week or season is over, fill in the pit completely.

12. At the latrine site, place the toilet paper roll in an old coffee can with a snap-top lid, and it will stay dry even in rain or snow. You can also fashion a privacy screen in front of the latrine with a 6- by 8-foot piece of nylon tarp tied between two or three saplings and anchored with rocks.

13. What's the one thing most hunters crave after two or three days afield? A shower! A makeshift shower can be created at little expense. Buy a plastic, collapsible 5-gallon water jug at a sporting goods store. Then go to a hardware store and buy a shower-head that has an on-off handle and is attached to a flexible 3-foot hose. Attach it to the water jug's filler spout. The jug can be filled with water, then lifted into the low fork of a nearby tree trunk so the water will gravity-feed to the showerhead. In mild temperatures, let the jug sit on a flat rock in sunlight; the water will become lukewarm in two hours. In cooler weather, a water jug that's been spray-painted flat black will absorb maximum heat from the sun, although still only to a lukewarm temperature. Some types of similar shower jugs are now also commercially available.

14. You can fashion a privacy screen around the shower in the same manner as the one made for your latrine, except taller. If you install it on slightly sloping ground, water will drain away from the shower stall, but it's still wise to have a rubber mat on the ground so you don't have to stand on mud when you bathe.

15. Precooked meals frozen in 1-gallon paper milk cartons simplify eating time. Since they're frozen, they'll eliminate the need for ice in your coolers for other food items. In days to come, they'll

Precooked, one-pot meals made at home and frozen in gallon-sized containers make dinners fast and easy.

begin to slowly defrost. To prepare, simply dump the contents into a large pot and heat.

Ideal meal items for this method include stews, hearty soups, noodle dishes with gravy, pork and beans, various meats such as chicken and pork, spaghetti, marzetti, chili, and ham and beans. Ask each hunter in your group to bring two or three precooked dishes that are already frozen and ready to travel.

16. Dishwashing after meals is fast and easy if each hunter in camp has brought a nylon mesh bag capable of holding one place setting. The dishwashing area should have three stations. The first one is where the plates are scraped clean of leftover food. The second station, with a large pot of boiling soapy water on the camp stove or over the fire, is where each diner sloshes his mesh bag of dinnerware and utensils up and down until they're clean. Then he moves to the third station, a pot of clean boiling water, where he dunks the bag several times to rinse his dishware. The mesh bag can be hung by its drawstring from a tree branch or a hook to drip-dry. One individual is then assigned to hand-wash any pots and pans used to cook the meal, and they're placed on paper toweling to drip-dry; this chore should be rotated each day among those in camp.

Dishwashing is a breeze if each hunter uses a nylon mesh bag and the popular double-dunk method.

17. Bring some old throw rugs to your tent camp and place one at the entrance to each tent. Now everyone can wipe his boots outside and not track snow and mud inside.

18. Add more gusto and variety to your dinner dishes by having a variety of spices and seasonings on hand. At home, transfer small quantities from larger containers into 35mm film canisters with snap-top lids. Your assortment can be kept together in a plastic bag with a zipper-lock closure. Be sure to include garlic powder, red cayenne pepper, onion powder, parsley flakes, oregano, dill, paprika, cinnamon, basil leaves, rosemary, thyme, and sage.

19. If you prefer liquefied gas for operating camp stoves and lanterns, use propane rather than butane. In cold weather—below 30°F—butane is difficult to ignite.

20. When an individual fills his tag and his hunt is over, most deer camps immediately award him the titles of Camp Cook, Dish-

A happy deer camp, and the success of its hunters, hinges upon the personalities. Of course, bucks like this would make anyone smile!

washer Emeritus, Chief Water Hauler, and Firewood Superintendent. By taking over these duties, the successful hunter lets his partners devote their energies solely to the pursuit of their own deer.

21. The success of a hunting camp hinges upon the personalities of those invited. If half the group wants to sit on stands and the other half insists on staging drives all day, there's sure to be discord. Similarly, if one or two individuals are burdened with all of the cooking and dishwashing chores while the others can't be coaxed away from the poker table, resentment can occur. It can take years to fine-tune the people chemistry of the annual deer hunting camp.

22. It's also customary in most deer camps that the hunter who fills his tag first contributes a small portion of his deer—most often the liver and heart—to that evening's celebratory dinner. Moreover, a standard rule is that *everyone* takes home venison, even if he didn't take a deer; in other words, those who successfully took deer share a portion of their venison with those who did not.

With five deer on the meat pole, every one in this camp is going home with a lot of venison.

23. If your hunt is going to span more than three or four days, and particularly if the weather is terrible and the terrain formidable, there's no logic to hunting long and hard from daylight to dark with everyone dragging tail. Instead, take a lunch break back in camp; a midday nap will allow all of you to keep going strong and remain in high spirits.

24. It's easy for a cabin or tent to become overcrowded with each hunter's personal belongings. But if each hunter brings several coolers for his personal gear, floor space remains clear and open; some of the coolers can even be placed outside if their contents aren't affected by freezing temperatures.

25. When tent camping, the annual deer hunting group should consider making use of two tents. One is reserved strictly for sleeping, changing clothes, and storage of personal gear. The other should be used for cooking, eating, socializing, and storage of communal gear. Pitch the tents so they're only 8 feet apart, with their front entranceways facing each other. This allows their

A work table outside the tent lets you accomplish a lot of chores without getting in each other's way.

two awnings to be tied together into an overhead canopy that will keep the connecting walkway dry during bad weather.

26. To maximize the interior space of a small cabin and make it seem more spacious, screw dozens of hooks onto the walls to hold clothing and miscellaneous lightweight gear that would otherwise get piled onto beds, chairs, tabletops, and even the floor. Any equipment that's weatherproof (fuel cans, tree stands, coolers) should be left outside in pickup beds or equipment trailers. You can also leave equipment that isn't totally weatherproof outside if you cover it with a tarp or store it in a temporary lean-to.

27. When you're cooking and eating outside a cabin or tent camp in mild to warm weather, you'll find that yellow jackets, deerflies, blackflies, and other insects can become bothersome. Solve the problem by filling an old tin can with water, stirring in a tablespoon of sugar, and placing it 20 feet away from your cooking and eating area. The insects will focus their attention on the syrupy treat and leave you and your partners alone.

28. If it's impractical to haul 5-gallon jugs of water to camp, don't drink stream or lake water without first treating it with Halazone tablets (available at any pharmacy). If you run out of the tablets, bring a pot of stream water to a rolling boil for five minutes. Then allow it to cool. If the taste is too flat, pour the water back and forth from one pot to another to replace the oxygen that the boiling removed.

29. When you're shopping for a new sleeping bag, keep in mind that synthetic linings may improve wicking and comfort in be-

If you must use stream water for drinking and cooking, boil it to make it safe.

low-freezing conditions, but in milder weather they collect more sweat and odors. Down yields more warmth for its weight and bulk, but synthetics handle dampness better. For mild weather (50°F and warmer), a sleeping bag with 2 pounds of filler material is usually sufficient. For moderately cold weather (50°F down to 20°F), 3 or 4 pounds of insulation is usually adequate. For very cold weather (from 20° to below 0°F), a bag of at least 5 pounds is a must.

30. Check every item of equipment before going to deer camp. Late at night on a mountainside in the dim glow of a flashlight is not the best way to read the instructions on how to set up a new tent.

31. In tents and unheated cabins, the kerosene heaters now on the market are safe and a joy to use. I've been in tent camps where the outside temperature was below 0°F, while inside we enjoyed supper in shirtsleeves and stocking feet. Pick a heater that has an automatic shut-off feature in case the unit is accidentally

A lightweight, compact kerosene heater with an automatic safety shut-off feature will keep a tent interior at 70°F even when it's below 0°F outside.

bumped or tipped over. When you transport the heater to and from camp, protect it by storing it in its original heavy-duty cardboard box with interior foam "bumpers." Before going to sleep at night, crack open a couple of windows or tent flaps for ventilation. *Always* keep the fuel can outside the tent, at least 20 yards away, and *always* refuel the heater outside the tent.

32. To optimize a wall tent's living space, bring to camp some coat hangers and large safety pins. The pins can be secured through the tent's sidewalls (not the ceiling canvas, or the pinholes will leak rainwater), and garments on hangers can then be stowed out of the way.

33. If your cabin or intended campsite isn't far from home, visit it a week or two before opening day. Now's the time to get everything ready so that everyone can focus on planning deer hunting strategies once the season starts. Replace the broken hinge on the outhouse door or dig a new latrine pit. Cut and stack

firewood and cover it with a tarp to keep it dry; green wood won't have time to season and burn properly, so look for dead, blowdown trees. Repair the leaky roof. Check the sturdiness of the meat pole and replace it if necessary. If security is no problem, you can even set up tents in advance, bring in your 5-gallon water jugs, and set up your tree stands and ground blinds.

34. Washing clothes in camp is easy. There will already be heavy-duty plastic bags, liquid soap (also for washing dishes), and assorted lengths of rope in camp. Simply remember to bring a handful of clothespins. Put several items of clothing in one bag along with 2 gallons of water and about a tablespoon of soap. Now tie the neck of the bag closed with a twist-tie and "massage" and agitate the contents of the bag as if you're kneading bread. Five minutes of this should be sufficient. Remove the clothes, wring out the soapy water, and place them in a second plastic bag containing 2 gallons of clean rinsewater; again, agitate the contents of the bag for five minutes. Finally, remove the clothes, wring them out, and hang them on your makeshift clothesline to drip-dry.

35. Don't let trash accumulate around camp; instead, dispose of it daily. Waxed paper, plastic bags, paper containers, and cardboard boxes can be burned in the fire ring outside your cabin or tent. And biodegradable items such as frying-pan grease, steak bones, and food scraps can be dumped into a shallow pit and covered with several shovelfuls of dirt. All that should remain are food tins, cans, and used aluminum foil, which can be rinsed, crushed, and placed in heavy-duty trash bags for the trip home.

36. Gasoline and propane lanterns are useless if their fragile silk mantles become broken. Always have spares on hand. Tape one or two mantles, in their original packaging, to the bottom of each lantern.

37. Stoves and lanterns also have small generator tubes that become clogged over time. Have replacements on hand, along with a small box wrench to replace them. In a pinch, you may be able to use a pin to clean the tiny orifice of a generator tube enough to coax a few more hours of usage out of it.

38. Gasoline stoves and lanterns will fail to hold fuel-tank pressure if the small leather cup at the end of the plunger rod inside the

plunger tube becomes dried out. Once dried, it will no longer provide a tight seal. Simply unscrew the plunger handle to remove it from its tube, then work a bit of cooking or motor oil into the leather with your fingertips to soften it and increase its size.

39. To keep their assorted cooking gear organized, many deer camp members build kitchen boxes from ¼-inch plywood. The materials are inexpensive, and the work can be completed in a couple of evenings. Cooking utensils, silverware, plates, cups, dishwashing tubs, pots and pans, and food items such as boxes of pasta, crackers, cookies, dried soup mixes, and the like go into the box. This system works much better than randomly stashing flimsy cardboard boxes and grocery bags throughout the camp.

CHAPTER
18

54 Ways to Ensure Succulent Venison

How to care for your animal from field to table.

1. Eat venison for better health. Venison has 10 percent fewer calories than an equal-sized portion of roast chicken or turkey and 50 percent fewer calories than ham or beef. The fat content of venison is only one-sixth that of beef. The cholesterol content of venison is comparable with chicken and turkey. Moreover, venison has more protein than fish, beef, chicken, turkey, or liver. It's also a rich source of iron, potassium, calcium, magnesium, zinc, and phosphorus—the primary trace elements found in mineral supplements.

2. One reason not to shoot at a deer that has been spooked and is running hard is that one's shot placement probably won't be accurate, and many of the animal's prime cuts of meat may be ruined. This is why the lung shot at a standing or slowly moving animal always is recommended; when properly made, the result is a quick kill with no valuable meat damaged.

3. A deer that has been wounded will have undergone a great deal of stress before you recover it. This means that adrenaline and lactic acid will have saturated its muscles. Conversely, when a deer is killed quickly and cleanly, its venison will have a sweet, clean flavor not contaminated by various waste residues.

4. When you recover your deer, the first order of business is to field-dress it so the meat can begin to cool. A knife with a 4-inch blade is recommended.

Begin field-dressing your deer as soon as possible so the carcass will begin cooling.

5. Ignore the old tale about immediately cutting off the deer's tarsal glands. When a deer dies, its glands become inactive and cannot contaminate the meat. Besides, they're located far from the main body trunk where the venison is. If you cut at the glands, you'll transfer tarsal scent to your knife blade and hands; if you then begin other field-dressing chores without washing your hands and knife, you will indeed contaminate the meat.

6. Avoid cutting the deer's throat. There's no need to bleed the animal; all of the blood will have collected in the chest cavity and will drain out when you open the animal. Besides, if it's a nice buck and you ruin the neck skin, a taxidermist can't do an acceptable mounting job.

7. With the deer on its back, and its head slightly uphill, open the animal's body cavity from just above the penis to the base of the sternum. Do this by lifting up the abdominal skin and using your knife with the blade facing up to make a *shallow* incision. Keep it shallow so that you don't puncture the underlying intestines and cause their contents to spill all over.

8. As the abdominal incision is completed, the paunch and intestines will begin to bulge up and out. Pull them out until you come to the diaphragm. This is a sheetlike wall of thin skin inside the body cavity that separates the lower abdominal organs from those in the chest region. Cut the diaphragm free by running your knife blade in a circular fashion around the entire inside perimeter of the chest cavity, to expose the lungs and heart.

9. Roll your sleeves up to your elbows and reach as far as possible up into the chest cavity. Now feel for the twin-tube esophagus and windpipe, sever it, and begin pulling it backward, making just a few judicious cuts here and there so the heart and lungs will pull out easily. Sever the heart from its restraining ligaments and set it aside.

10. Next, sever the liver from its attachment to the abdominal organs, and set it aside as well.

11. With the chest and abdominal organs removed, now work on the excretory organs by extending your incision to the base of the penis (or, if it's a doe, make a shallow, oval cut around the udder and remove that flap of skin). Since the penis and testi-

cles lie on top of the abdomen, a shallow cut around them will allow them to be removed.

12. Extend the incision to the anus, encircling the anus with the tip of your knife blade (or, if it's a doe, go around the entire anus/vagina area). This will create a flap of skin around the orifice that you can pull on as you gradually cut deeper and deeper around its diameter, moving into the pelvic canal to free the rectum. Exposing this work area is easier if a friend pulls back on the hind legs to lift the rump area; if you're alone, push back the legs with one of your shoulders.

13. When you reach the point at which the rectum has been entirely freed, stop working from this direction and begin coming in the remainder of the way from the other (abdominal) side. Push away as much lower intestine as possible and begin separating the bladder from inside the pelvic canal.

14. The bladder is a small, pouchlike organ. If it's only partially filled with urine, it won't present any problems. If it's full and distended, however, you have to be careful that it doesn't spill inside the cavity. Pinch the ureter tightly closed with your fingertips. Slice it free, then aim it away from the deer and exert gentle hand pressure on the bladder to release the urine spray away from your work area. Now tie the ureter closed with a piece of string and continue cutting the bladder from within the pelvic canal. Cuts made from this direction will eventually meet those made from the anus side, and you'll be able to pull out the entire reproductive/excretory tract in one long, undamaged string.

15. Bacteria is the primary cause of meat spoilage. Remove all the moisture remaining in the body cavity as soon as possible, so there are no breeding grounds available for bacterial growth.

16. With the deer's insides removed, roll the carcass onto its belly, with the animal's front and rear legs spread-eagled. Now grab the antlers and shake the carcass as you slowly drag it forward. This will free clotted blood and lymph fluids that, if left in the body cavity, would quickly cause the spoiling process to begin.

17. Flip the carcass back onto its back and use handfuls of clean, dry grass, ferns, or moss to swab out the cavity and mop up any remaining surface moisture.

18. If the deer cannot be immediately removed from the field, don't leave it on its side, because body heat won't be able to escape from the carcass. Instead, roll the deer onto its back and insert several sticks crosswise in the abdominal region to keep the cavity as open as possible.

19. If you have trouble keeping the deer's carcass on its back, brace it with a log or rocks, or lean it against a stump or tree trunk.

20. If there's a chance that birds or coyotes may begin eating the carcass while you're returning to camp to enlist help in dragging the deer, don't leave until you've hung an article of clothing on a nearby tree branch. A T-shirt that reeks of human scent and is fluttering in the breeze will usually ward away scavengers.

21. If the weather is warm, and there will be a delay in removing the deer to camp, drag the carcass a short distance to a north-facing slope or into a thick stand of conifers. In either location, the shade and somewhat lower air temperature will help the carcass cool.

22. The heart and liver can be carried out immediately. Most hunters keep a couple of plastic bags in their fanny pack for this very purpose.

23. At home or in camp, it's preferable to hang a deer in a *protected* location such as an unheated building in which the doors and windows can be closed to keep out any scavengers. If this isn't possible, select a shaded location such as an open-air shed or a meat pole in a stand of conifers and hang the deer high out of reach of animals.

24. In warm weather, don't hang a deer by the antlers because body heat rising from the hind legs and abdominal region will be trapped in the chest cavity, preventing it from cooling rapidly.

25. Hang the deer by the hind legs with a gambrel inserted into slits cut between the hocks and Achilles tendons. With the deer in this position, body heat from the neck, chest, and abdominal region can quickly escape.

26. Trim away bloodied, unwanted skin and fat globs around the field-dressing incision, throughout the chest, and through the abdominal and pelvic cavities.

Hang your deer with a rope and a gambrel inserted through the Achilles tendons.

27. Pour a cup of salt into a pail of water and, using a clean hand towel that has been thoroughly wrung out, swab the inside of the body cavity; be sure to reach as far as possible up into the chest and neck region. This will remove any dried blood, as well as dirt or other debris that got into the cavity when you were dragging out the deer. Now use a dry towel to dry the inside of the body cavity. The ribs should literally glisten.

28. Whether a deer is allowed to hang in camp or at home, the carcass should be continually protected from blowflies and insects, which can ruin the venison in short order. But forget the old advice about sprinkling black pepper onto the carcass. You'd need at least 5 pounds, and the wind would blow most of it away. It's much better to use a porous, tightly woven cloth game bag made for this purpose that encloses the deer in a co-

If the temperature is warm, remove the animal's hide to assist the cooling process, then enclose the carcass in a cloth game bag.

coon. The better ones cost as much as $25 apiece but can be washed and reused.

29. When should you remove the deer's hide? Let the air temperature determine that. As a rule, if the average daily temperature is above 45°F, the hide should come off as soon as possible, to ensure rapid cooling of the venison; butchering should take place immediately thereafter. If the temperature is consistently below 40°F, the hide can generally remain on for as long as you want the venison to age.

30. If the temperature is consistently below 32°F and the carcass is allowed to freeze, it becomes extremely difficult to remove the hide and then attend to other rough-butchering chores. Also, a cardinal rule in meat handling is never to allow meat to alternately freeze and thaw. In this situation, it's best to remove the hide before the carcass freezes, then butcher it into primal cuts (rear legs, front legs, saddle, neck). If you're in a tent camp, the cuts can then be wrapped in white butcher's paper and placed in coolers, which will help prevent the meat from freezing even

if the temperature dips into the teens. It would be even better to have access to a building where the coolers can be stored.

31. If the temperature is warm (above 45°F) and you have a long drive home, wrap the primal cuts of venison in butcher's paper and place them in camping coolers on top of bags of ice. At each rest stop, take a moment to open the coolers' drain plugs to remove any meltwater that has begun to accumulate before it can begin contacting the venison.

32. If the deer head and hide are thoroughly salted down and placed in heavy-duty plastic trash bags, they'll require no further attention until they can be delivered to a taxidermist.

33. Aging a deer carcass imparts both flavor and tenderness. The ideal aging temperature is 36° to 38°F, and the ideal length of time to age venison is five to seven days. If it's too hot or too cold to age the carcass outside, reduce it to primal cuts, wrap the cuts in white butcher's paper, and place them in a refrigerator's lower compartment where the temperature can be controlled. After the primal cuts have aged in the fridge, they can be butchered into meal-sized portions, wrapped, and transferred to the freezer.

34. When processing their own deer, most hunters prefer to bone out the meat rather than create various cuts with a meat saw. This way they don't fill valuable freezer space with 40 pounds of bones. Using a saw also sprinkles marrow dust from the bones throughout the meat and can give the venison an off flavor.

35. Venison's occasional gamy taste is usually the result of tallow (fat) that was not completely trimmed away after the boned-out cuts were created. The fat from domestic animals imparts a pleasant flavor to their meat, but that's not the case with wild animals, so try to remove as much as possible.

36. Most venison chefs prefer to process their deer carcass so that the boned-out backstraps from the saddle are cut into 1-inch-thick steaks that can be fried or grilled. The back legs are reduced to their individual large muscle groups for use as pot roasts, or are cut into 1-inch-thick slices to be used as Swiss steak. The front legs and neck are generally the toughest and

Remove as much of the fat as possible when cutting up your deer.

are reserved for stew meat, burger, and sausage. The ribs can be slow-cooked in a pressure cooker or Crock-Pot, then briefly transferred to a charcoal grill and basted with barbecue sauce.

37. When properly double-wrapped, venison steaks and roasts will remain in good condition in a freezer for two years; the first wrap should be plastic wrap, which tightly clings to irregular meat surfaces to make an airtight enclosure. The second wrap should be heavy freezer paper to protect each package from coming into contact with other freezer items. Seal each package with freezer tape and be sure to label and date the contents. To retain the meat's flavor, always slowly defrost venison overnight in your refrigerator; don't allow it to sit on a sink drainboard, at room teperature.

38. How can venison remain in a freezer in good condition for as long as two years when beef and pork have a recommended storage life of only four to six months? It's because beef and pork are high in fat, and it's the fat in meat that becomes rancid and shortens freezer life. Lean venison has almost no marbling, however, and knowledgeable hunters carefully trim away all the exterior fat. Thus, there's nothing to spoil.

39. If the venison you've defrosted for a meal has a bit of freezer burn around the edges, don't worry: It's nothing more than mi-

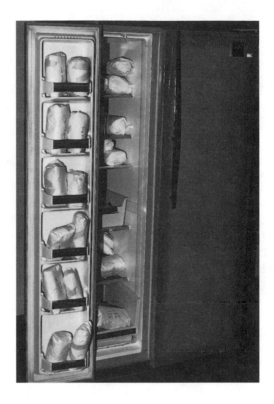

If the cuts of venison have been trimmed of all fat and are wrapped in airtight packages, the frozen meat will remain in good condition for two years.

nor discoloration and surface drying due to the low humidity in the freezer. Trim it away and there will be good, pure meat underneath.

40. Unlike venison steaks and roasts, venison burger and sausage should be used within four to six months. The making of burger and sausage involves the addition of beef or pork fat, and that dramatically shortens freezer life.

41. To correctly freeze wrapped packages of venison and so ensure their longevity, don't overload your freezer's flash-freezing ability by putting in all the packages at once. Turn the temperature dial down to 0°F and place only a few of the packages in the freezer at a time so they'll freeze quickly and solidly. Put more packages into the freezer every three hours, storing the remaining packages in a refrigerator in the meantime. When your entire cache of venison is frozen rock-solid, you can return the freezer's temperature dial to its normal setting of 20°F. If you were to place all your venison packages in the freezer at once and fail to turn the temperature down to 0°F, they wouldn't

freeze quickly, leading to the formation of ice crystals on the meat. When eventually defrosted, the venison would likely have a mushy texture and unfresh flavor.

42. To properly defrost venison, don't let it sit on the drainboard of a kitchen sink at room temperature. Take it out of the freezer the night before you plan to cook it and allow it to slowly defrost in your refrigerator.

43. The recommended ratio for creating burger is 4 parts venison to 1 part beef suet or fat. First, grind the burger and suet separately. Then, using a flat, clean work surface, thoroughly mix the ground venison and suet with your hands. Grind it a second time.

44. The recommended ratio for bulk sausage is 3 parts venison to 1 part beef suet and 1 part lean pork. First, grind the venison, suet, and pork separately. Then, on a flat, clean work surface, thoroughly mix the ground venison, suet, and pork with your hands. Grind it a second time. Next, evenly spread the ground mixture back on your work surface to a thickness of about 1 inch. Sprinkle the sausage seasoning of your choice on top of the mixture—prepared sausage-seasoning blends (hot, mild, Italian, sage, and others) are available in most grocery stores. Thoroughly knead the mixture with your hands and run it through your grinder a third time. The sausage mixture should then be placed in a large bowl or wrapped in paper and put in your refrigerator for at least 24 hours to allow the seasoning flavors to permeate the meat. A day later, reduce the sausage mixture to smaller meal-sized portions, wrap it, and freeze it.

Many hunters prefer to grind their own burger and sausage. It's easy, especially if you have an electric grinder. Add beef fat to the venison to make burger, or beef fat, lean pork, and seasonings to make sausage.

The Whitetail Deer Hunter's Almanac

Prepared sausage-seasoning mixes can be obtained at most grocery stores.

45. You can also take the portion of your venison intended for sausage to a processor. Have casings stuffed and made into links and rounds of summer sausage, Polish sausage, pepperoni, kielbasa, bologna, or salami.

46. Since venison looks very much like beef, some people make the mistake of trying to cook it like beef, usually with disastrous results. Venison is dry and lean; it lacks beef's marbling, which is what breaks down the tissue fibers during cooking and makes the meat tender. So venison steaks should never be cooked to more than medium-rare or they'll be as tough as boot leather. There are several exceptions, such as burger and sausage; because fat has been added to these, they can be cooked to well done if desired. Similarly, the creation of soups

Never cook venison beyond medium-rare, or the meat will become tough.

Lesser cuts of venison such as round steaks can be made tender by braising.

and stews typically sees the venison slow-cooked in some type of liquid (broth, stock, water, wine, juice), which permeates the meat and has a tenderizing effect.

47. With other cuts of venison, such as Swiss steaks, round steaks, and roasts, other tenderizing methods are in order, especially if the venison is from an older deer. Commercial meat tenderizers, available in any grocery store, are suitable for lesser cuts such as round and sirloin-tip steaks.

48. Steaks can also be braised, which means they are floured, browned in oil, and seared on both sides in a hot frying pan. The heat is then reduced to very low and several cups of water or broth are added. Let the meat slow-cook for 45 minutes.

49. Roasts can be layered with strips of bacon on top, or they can be soaked overnight in a marinade before roasting. Then insert a meat thermometer into the thickest part of the roast and bake at 350°F until the meat's temperature registers 145°F (no more!). It will be fork-tender.

50. Steaks and roasts can also be prepared in a pressure cooker or slow-cooked in a Crock-Pot.

51. The tenderloins (not to be confused with the backstraps along the outside of the spine) are the most tender part of the deer. They're located inside the body cavity along the spine. Most

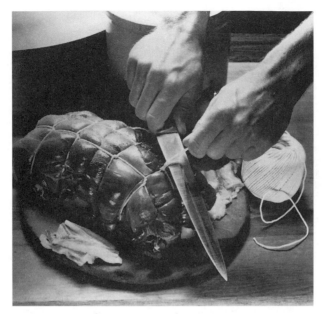

Large cuts of venison such as a rump roast can be oven-baked to perfection.

hunters traditionally sear them in a hot frying pan for several minutes on each side until medium-rare, then slice them thinly for steak sandwiches smothered with sautéed onions and peppers. The tenderloins also are terrific in Oriental stir-fry recipes.

52. Venison liver and heart can be cooked just like beef liver and heart.

53. Always serve your venison on a hot serving platter, and remember to preheat the dinner plates. The reason is that venison doesn't have hot marbling fat within its tissue fibers to keep the meat warm. If you put it on a cold serving platter straight from the cupboard, and then transfer it to cold dinner plates, the meat will quickly cool—becoming tougher and tougher in the process.

54. Every hunter should have at least one wild-game cookbook he can regularly consult for a wide variety of ideas and recipes specifically designed for venison.